THE GODS
OF REBIRTH

THE GODS OF REBIRTH

THE MYTHOLOGY OF MODERN MAGIC

NEVILL DRURY

PRISM · UNITY

Originally published in Great Britain 1973 as *The Path of the Chameleon* by Neville Spearman (Jersey) Limited

This edition published in Great Britain 1988 by:
PRISM PRESS
2 South Street,
Bridport,
Dorset DT6 3NQ

and distributed in the USA by:
AVERY PUBLISHING GROUP INC.,
350 Thorens Avenue,
Garden City Park,
New York 11040

and published in Australia 1988 by:
UNITY PRESS
6a Ortona Road,
Lindfield,
NSW 2070

ISBN 1 85327 011 3

© 1973, 1988 Nevill Drury

All rights reserved. No part of this publication may be reproduced, stored in a retrieval system, or transmitted, in any form or by any means, electronic, mechanical, photo-copying, recording or otherwise, without the prior permission of the publishers.

Printed and bound in the Channel Islands
by The Guernsey Press Limited.

This book is for my father

ACKNOWLEDGEMENTS

I would like to thank my wife Sue for her encouragement, and Mr. Ted Marriott and Mr. Serge Yalichev for their assistance with the photography. Thanks are also due to Mrs. Edna Skinner, Mrs. Joy Busby, Miss Shirley Astle and Miss Anne-Maree Phillips who typed the manuscript. I would like also to thank Mr. Stephen Skinner for providing important material on Moses and the Judaic tradition.

CONTENTS

Section I—APPROACHES. . . .
  I Magic, Religion and the Academic View   13
  II Avatars and Gnostikoi   38
  III The Symbolism of Magic   62

Section II—THE PATH OF THE CHAMELEON
  I The Egyptian Books of the Dead   81
  II Graeco-Roman Shamans and Journeys to the Underworld   103
  III The Chaldean Oracles   116
  IV The Qabalah and the Tree of Life   127
  V Neophyte, Zelator, Theoricus, Adept   135

Appendix A Archetypal Correspondences   145
Appendix B The Divine Names attributed to the Sephiroth   146

Bibliography   147

Index   150

"I have come by day, and I have risen in the footsteps of the gods...."
Papyrus of Nu

APPROACHES

CHAPTER ONE

Magic, Religion and the Academic View

Towards the end of his life the mystical French writer Gerard de Nerval commenced writing a prose work which began: 'Our dreams are a second life.' Further on in the work, which was titled *Aurelia* there occurs the following passage:

> '. . . I was really only walking in the empire of shadows. My companions around me seemed to be asleep and to resemble spectres of Tartarus, until the hour at which the sun rose for me. Then I greeted that luminary with a prayer, and my real life began. From that moment on, when I felt sure that I was being subjected to the tests of a sacred initiation, an invincible strength entered my soul. I imagined myself a hero living under the gaze of the gods; everything in Nature took on a new aspect . . .'[1]

Initiation refers to the transformation of man into something greater than he was before, an acquisition of new meaning through the realization that he is more than dust and shadow. This is the essential element of the Mystery Teachings of Eleusis, the doctrine of the 'second-birth' or the 'new-awakening' in religion, and the implied symbolic meaning of the Phoenix rising from the ashes.

Today, especially among the young, there has been a turning from science to the realm of Pan, a marked trend away from the precise and the defined, towards what has been hitherto re-

[1] Gerard de Nerval: *Selected Writings*. Panther Books, 1968.

garded as irrational; the world of the unconscious, the realm of magic and secret symbols. It is possible that the incursion of a largely anonymous urban existence in Western Society has brought with it a quest for origins and meaning, where the individual is not felt to be merely a social unit but a *being*. It is in the study of exotic magical and religious tracts, whether it be the *I Ching*, the *Qabalah*, the *Tarot*, or the *Egyptian* and *Tibetan Books of the Dead*, that proof of man's true dignity is at present being sought. Social theorists and psychologists have not yet had time to analyse in depth the most recent advent of esoteric doctrines within our society, but the old theories about 'superstition' still stand. Despite this fact, the world of magic and occult teachings (until now, a minority interest in the West) has failed to subside, and has never in truth ever been defeated. At certain times in history, it has been less in currency than at others when it has appeared in strength: times like the Middle Ages when it took various forms—the Qabalistic revival of Gnostic mysticism, spiritual alchemy, and even witchcraft with its pagan survivals; the turn of the twentieth century, when it flourished in the form of ritual derived from Qabalistic, Egyptian and Rosicrucian sources in groups like the Golden Dawn; and finally the present day, where there has been an extraordinary revival of techniques of manipulating the consciousness whether by meditation, drugs, posture and breathing exercises, fasting, etc.

Naturally occultism has a lot to say about these things. It has known them longer than science, and has developed them into techniques. Whereas science deals with empirically observable causes and effects, occultism deals pragmatically with methods of altering consciousness to produce certain effects. One of these is the assimilation within the self of the characteristics of a deity in ceremonial ritual (identification with a God),[2] another is the separation of consciousness from the physical body in what

---

[2] A deity represents a force higher than that of man, and consequently such identification is a transcendental act.

Celia Green has recently termed the 'ecsomatic', (or 'out-of-the-body') experience.[3]

Modern occultism has many antecedents and is the result of the fusion of many pantheons and traditions. The academic analysis of the religious and the magical has up till now been the domain of two main disciplines, anthropology and psychology. Broadly speaking the anthropologist is interested in how a religious or a magical belief manifests in society, a psychologist is interested in the source of the manifestation, whether it be the result of childhood experiences as Freud thought, or of archaic images from the depths of the unconscious as in the theory of Jung. Today both schools have moved away from the analysis of magico-religious origins, the anthropologists finding more fruit for research in purely social phenomena. Psychology, which like anthropology, has long been plagued by problems of definition in dealing with intangibles like 'culture' and 'the mind' has tended to adopt a more empirical stance in behaviouristic models, in a somewhat desperate attempt to become 'truly scientific'.

In anthropological research there has been in recent years, a falling off of original methods of approach. As Clifford Geertz puts it, the study 'is in fact in a state of general stagnation', probably due to a lack of specific returns. Quite rightly Evans-Pritchard has observed that one can hardly waste time in the vain pursuit of the origins of magic and religion. These are lost to antiquity and can only be the source of endless unprovable hypotheses. In addition, one of the basic difficulties encountered by anthropologists is the essential lack of certainty over what constitutes magical or religious phenomena in the first place. Many anthropologists tend to regard the two together, on the basis of their supranormal aspects, but usually magic is regarded as being more involved with specific results. John Middleton has drawn the distinction as follows: 'We may say that the realm of magic is that in which human beings believe that they may directly affect nature and each other for good or ill, by

[3] Referred to, when voluntary, as astral projection.

their own efforts (even though the precise mechanism may not be understood by them) as distinct from appealing to divine powers by sacrifice or prayer' (religion).[4]

The early definition by Tylor that religion was characterised by belief in superhuman beings still finds currency in a recent essay by Melford Spiro, who writes that the belief in such beings 'and in their power to assist or to harm men, approaches universal distribution'. We find similar beings in both primitive magic and mythology, where the gods are often personifications of natural phenomena, like the sun, moon, rain, river, etc.—and also in modern ritual magic where Judaic archangels (Raphael, Gabriel, Michael and Uriel) have been adapted for specific purposes of invocation.

Anthropologists have isolated various reasons for the occurrence and persistence of magic and religion within society and these are as follows. Broadly speaking both magical and religious beliefs are said to provide the semblance of order in a world which often appears to us to be variable, unjust, chaotic and unmeaningful. In particular, religion provides the world with meaning by asserting the existence of a valid code of ethics and morals, an after-life earned in this one, etc., and also allows us to believe in a greater authority than that provided by mere men. The God-figure is seen as a personage whose will is interpreted so that man can look beyond his narrow social confines and act in a way which fulfils a greater, and possibly even 'divine', purpose. Malinowski, writing cynically, has emphasized that religion helps one to endure 'situations of emotional stress by opening up escapes from such situations and impasses as offer *no empirical way out* except by ritual and belief into the domain of the supernatural'.[5] Geertz, adopting a less escapist explanation mentions that by means of religion the everyday experience is 'transformed' for the individual into

---

[4] John Middleton (ed.): *Magic, Witchcraft and Curing.* Natural History Press, New York, 1967 p.x.

[5] Bronislaw Malinowski: *Magic, Science and Religion.* Beacon Press, Boston 1948, p. 67.

something more intelligible (even if, as in Geertz's opinion, religion isn't really 'true'): 'The existence of bafflement, pain and moral paradox—of the problem of meaning—is one of the things that drive men toward belief in gods, devils, spirits. . . .'[6] Philosopher Santayana has made much the same point in stating that 'another world to live in . . . is what we mean by having a religion'. For many this 'other world' is what constitutes the sacred.

Magic similarly has recourse to rituals and ceremonies of 'transformation' as in those initiation ceremonies in primitive society whereby the individual receives new knowledge from the elders about his true role in society, or secrets about the Dreamtime. In modern Qabalistic magic, greater self-knowledge is provided by systematic exploration of the unconscious and the experience of visions.[7]

Anthropologists on the whole have been reluctant to step beyond the social aspects of religion. Thus they analyse the way in which a totem animal symbolizes the unity of a clan of natives, or the way in which a shaman or medicine man can wield power over subordinates by allegedly resorting to mysterious techniques and sources of authority which no one else has access to. Spiro, in acknowledging the necessity of some psychological explanations of both religion and magic has stated that the 'pursuit of nirvana or heaven reduces our anxiety about the persistence of existence and can also transcend the problem of human suffering by regarding the world as essentially sinful, frustrating or evil. . . .'[8] Ritual, even if it doesn't work, can reduce the feeling of anxiety and helplessness and therefore has 'an important psychological function'. Thus, a deity so far as Spiro is concerned, is something dependable, to be relied upon in a time of crisis.

Sigmund Freud, who among psychologists has influenced

[6] Clifford Geertz: 'Religion as a Cultural System'. A.S.A.5 Tavistock, London 1966, p. 25.
[7] More Specifically, Tattvic Visions, Path Workings, and Rising on the Planes.
[8] Melford E. Spiro: 'Religion; Problems of Definition and Explanation. A.S.A.5 Tavistock, London, 1966, p. 102.

Spiro and other anthropologists extensively, believed that religion as a cure for anxiety had its origin in the family and specifically in childhood experiences. A child, Freud argued, observed his parents as either benevolent or malevolent depending on whether they were friendly, provided or withheld food, seemed 'powerful', etc. and these distinctions were taken later as the basis of magical and religious beliefs. In Freud's view, a god is no more than an enlarged version of a childish perception. In addition, he held that there were three essential stages of growth in an individual: narcissism (self-centeredness), dependence on the parents, and maturity. Freud, keen to draw parallels, correlated these psychological stages with magical, religious and scientific belief respectively. A person who believed in magic or religion, could hardly be said, in Freud's view, to be a fully developed person. This parallels an earlier theory propounded by Sir James Frazer, author of *The Golden Bough*, that all societies went through three stages, the magical, the religious and the scientific, as a natural process of evolution. This theory is no longer acceptable, but understandably Frazer was writing from the viewpoint of Victorian England priding itself on Imperial glory, 'cultural superiority' and a newly-established scientific rationale.

At this stage we can ask: What emerges from all these theories and analyses?

Are magic and religion in fact only ways of making one's view of the world more orderly and palatable? Are they only the upshoots of child experience projected on a large scale?

Firstly, it can be shown that there are many primitive societies where belief in supernatural beings causes extensive *fear* among the inhabitants and which are not conducive to security, but quite the opposite:

M. G. Marwick, who studied the Cewa tribe of Central Africa collected approximately two hundred cases of misfortunes, mostly deaths, of which he was able to analyse carefully 194. Of these only 25 per cent of deaths were attributed to natural causes (or acts of God) whereas 55 per cent of deaths were attributed to sorcery, mostly non-sorcerers being killed by sorcerers.

The supernatural universe of the Netsilik Eskimos of the Arctic coast of Canada is similarly filled mostly with malevolent beings. In this society, shamans have control of only one class of spirits called 'tunraqs' which it would appear occupy a roughly equivalent relationship to witches' familiars.[9] Some shamans have had trouble controlling their tunraqs,[10] and a tunraq which failed to achieve its task (murder, inflicting punishment, etc.) could often in blind fury, turn against its owner. This is not merely a case of people personifying their distrust or fear of a mysterious man, in the form of spirits, because the shamans 'interacted with the major dieties and played an important role in myth . . . shamans often appeared in essential myths such as those depicting the earliest time on earth, and the creation of mankind'.[11]

Among the Nyoro speaking natives of Bunyoro in Western Uganda, the ghosts of the dead are regarded as a constant threat, causing misfortune and illness which could only be allayed by getting a 'diviner' to deal with the offended ghost. Ghosts were generally regarded as troublesome because after a person died he ceased to think of his kin as 'his' people: 'the ghost no longer takes a warm and friendly human interest in the welfare of his living kin. . . .' Most of the ritual in this community is in fact aimed at keeping such ghosts at a distance. The worst ghosts of all don't even originate in the village but come 'from outside the household perhaps from very far away'. . . . 'These "nameless ghosts" may make impossible demands. . . .

---

[9] They were not however resident in animal bodies. Nevertheless 'tunraqs' usually remained in the vicinity of their 'owner', they liked to be frequently called and used—Asen Balikci 'Shamanistic Behaviour among the Netsilik Eskimos' in *Magic, Witchcraft and Curing*, Natural History. Press, New York, 1967, p. 191 et seq.

[10] One spirit called Orpingalik 'used to attack his master Anaidjug suddenly from behind and pull out his genitals; the unfortunate shaman after much yelling, could recover them during a trance'—Asen Balikci, p. 195.

[11] Asen Balikci, p. 205.

If (the ghost) doesn't get what it wants it may kill off a whole settlement'.[12]

Malevolent beings do not occur only among primitives. Certain branches of mysticism (especially 'emanationist' types where the Godhead manifests in the world in different stages) state that the soul, or disembodied psyche encounters various devils and demons after death. Sometimes they are conceived as being treacherous in their own right, and at other times illusory and conducive to misinterpretation. But they are *never* dependable.

Tibetan Buddhists have formulated an elaborate after-death belief in which the consciousness of the individual passes through various 'Bardo' visions which are a symbolic effect of his karma (good or evil deeds and their result) and a reflection of his own personality. One characteristic demon, or 'wrathful deity' is the Great Glorious Buddha-Heruka which appears on the eighth day after death.[13] 'Dark-brown of colour (it has) three heads, six hands, and four feet firmly postured, the right face being white, the left red, the central dark brown; the body emitting flames of radiance; the nine eyes widely opened in terrifying gaze; the eyebrows quivering like lightening, the protruding teeth glistening and set over one another . . . the heads adorned with dried (human) skulls and the symbols of the sun and moon, black serpents and raw (human) heads forming a garland for the body. . . .'[14]

The Gnostic sacred book which probably dates from the third century A.D. refers (Book 5, Chapter 139) to the entity 'Paraplex, a ruler with a woman's shape, whose hair reacheth down to her feet under whose authority stand five and twenty archdemons which rule over a multitude of other demons. It is those demons which enter into men and seduce

---

[12] John Beattie: 'Divination in Bunyoro, Uganda': *Magic, Witchcraft and Curing.* Natural History Press, New York, 1967.

[13] These 'days' are symbolic, not literal. The 'consciousness' spends 49 'days' in the after-life prior to the next incarnation.

[14] W. Y. Evans-Wentz: *The Tibetan Book of the Dead.* Oxford University Press, New York, 1960, p. 137.

them, raging and cursing and slandering; and it is they which carry off hence, and in ravishment, the souls, and dispatch them through their dark smoke and their evil chastisements.'[15]

There are also details of the 'Twelve dungeons of the Outer Darkness' which are ruled by creatures with strange names: Enchthonin (a crocodile), Charachar (a cat), Archaroch (a dog), Achrochar (a serpent), Marchur (a black bull), Lamchomor (a wild boar), Luchar (a bear), Laroch (a vulture), Archeoch (a basilisk), Xarmaroch (a being with a head of seven dragons), Rochar (a being with a head of seven cats) and Chremaor (a being with a head of seven dogs). (Bk. 4).

In both these cases (Buddhist and Gnostic) it is impossible to 'explain' the supernatural teachings as beliefs which 'unify society', or which 'provide security'. Both of these schools emphasise that *self-knowledge* is the key enabling the soul to pass such demons unhindered: mere belief is insufficient. In the Buddhist system such demons are recognised as illusions and figments of the imagination, albeit real enough to the disembodied consciousness. The Gnostics too, as their name suggests, emphasized secret, divine knowledge as the means of liberation from a world inherently tainted with evil; sacred words of power were able to dispel pernicious demons.

Freud's theory that child-experiences originate the religious or magical viewpoint would also seem open to doubt. Those types of religion where the Deity is seen to manifest in different and sometimes contradictory aspects, would appear to undermine his hypothesis.

For example, in the *Zohar*, the principal Qabalistic treatise which has as its central symbol the Tree of Life, the ten Sephiroth or emanations, from the tri-partite God-head (Ain, Ain Soph, Ain Soph Aur) align themselves in three pillars, which balance themselves in polarity into male, androgyne (male-female), and female. The first Sephirah, Kether, poten-

[15] G. R. S. Mead (ed.). *Pistis Sophia*. John Watkins, London, 1963.

tially contains both male and female elements[16] however, and certainly cannot be explained by reference to one parent *or* the other, as Freud's theory demands.

Freud derived his parental explanations within the context of the strongly patriarchal Viennese society of which he was a member. Correspondingly his simplistic evolutionary approach involving a linear progression from superstition to science is little more than a statement of Freud's own world view. It was not uncommon in the ethnology of the times to suppose that man had reached the social apex, and that magic was a symptom of an earlier cultural phase.

Freud's explanation of magic, then, is actually more a social than a psychological one despite appearances. The interfusion of anthropology and psychology had not yet occurred, and the question of the 'primitive mentality' was not seriously contemplated until the advent of Boas and Levy-Bruhl.

It would seem nevertheless that a great portion of belief, be it magical or religious, is not socially contrived, but does indeed manifest from the unconscious, the font of forgotten memories, repressed ideas, and basic primal energies.

More than any other psychologist, the man who had most to say about the mythological and magico-religious contents of the unconscious was Carl Jung. Beginning as a follower and colleague of Freud, Jung soon began to differ from Freud's interpretation of the unconscious psyche. Freud considered that the unconscious contained merely those infantile tendencies which had been repressed because the maturing adult found them 'incompatible'. Jung did not disagree with this as a characteristic of the unconscious, but considered it to be the only most obvious of a number of observable factors. For him the unconscious contained a vast storehouse of imagery which was much greater than the repressions of the individual. It also seemed to him that to a certain extent the unconscious appeared to act independently of the conscious mind.

---

[16] See A. E. Waite: *The Secret Doctrine in Israel.* O.M.T.B.C. Boston, 1914, especially Ch. XVII.

Most of Jung's hypotheses are derived from his analysis of dreams, which as a phenomenon had first been investigated at length by Freud who was himself initially interested in their relationship to *conscious* thoughts. Freud soon discovered however that when a patient was encouraged to discuss his dreams, he would uncover unconscious elements as well. Because these often reflected the origin of neuroses, the recognition by the patient of the unconscious elements had a therapeutic effect. Jung decided, however, that to allow the patient to discuss dreams at random would entail a moving away from the dream *per se*. For him each dream was in a sense complete within itself and 'expressed something specific that the unconscious was trying to say'.[17] Whereas Freud tended to uncover sexual motifs in dreams, Jung regarded the individual situation as foremost in solving the language of the dream, rather than attempting to identify fixed motifs like the phallus or breast. Jung writes: 'A man may dream of inserting a key in a lock, of wielding a heavy stick, or of breaking down a door with a battering ram. Each of these can be regarded as a sexual allegory. But the fact that his unconscious, for its own purposes, has chosen one of these specific images—it may be the key, the stick or the battering ram—is also of major significance. The real task is to understand why the key has been referred to the stick or the stick to the ram. And sometimes this might even lead one to discover that it is not the sexual act at all that is represented but some quite different psychological point. . . .'[18]

Jung came to the conclusion that the dream had 'its own limitation' and could not be manipulated so that a symbol meant the same thing in every dream. Nevertheless the dream was not a random occurrence but intrinsically made sense, if only its meaning could be discovered. The dream was 'a specific expression of the unconscious'.[19] And the reason why it was expressed at all said Jung, was that it was compensating for aspects of the personality which were unbalanced. An over-

[17] C. G. Jung: *Man and His Symbols*. Dell, New York, 1968, p. 12.
[18] Ibid., p. 13.   [19] Ibid., p. 18.

APPROACHES

egotistical person would frequently have dreams about symbolically 'coming down to earth' for example.

But there were also certain motifs within dreams which did not seem to Jung to be a part of the individual psyche. It was the study of these symbols which led him to formulate the concept of the 'collective unconscious'. 'There are many symbols', he wrote, 'that are not individual but collective in their nature and origin. These are chiefly religious images, their origin is so far buried in the mystery of the past that they seem to have no human source. But they are, in fact, "collective representations" emanating from primeval dreams and creative fantasies. As such, these images are involuntary spontaneous manifestations and by no means intentional inventions.'[20] What Jung is saying in effect is that at a certain psychic level motifs common to the whole of mankind are capable of manifesting in dreams. These motifs are a symbolic expression of 'the constantly repeated experiences of humanity,' that is to say they are derived from observations about nature (the sky, changes of season, etc.) which have become in a sense, imbedded in the psychic patterns of the whole human species.

Jung called these primordial images 'archetypes' and it is perhaps this aspect of his work which has aroused most controversy.[21] He gives the following example of how an archetype is formed: 'One of the commonest and at the same time most impressive experiences is the apparent movement of the sun every day. We certainly cannot discover anything of the kind in the unconscious, so far as the known physical process is concerned. What we do find on the other hand, is the myth of the sun hero in all its countless modifications. It is this *myth* and *not the physical process* that forms the sun archetype.'[22] Thus the

---

[20] Ibid., pp. 41–2.

[21] Much of this argument hinges around whether symbols have innate meaning. Claude Levi-Strauss, the influential French anthropologist has dismissed Jung's view because he believes that symbols only have meaning within their social context despite his concession that myths have a collective origin.

[22] C. G. Jung: *Two Essays on Analytical Psychology*. Routledge & Kegan Paul, London, 1953, p. 68.

archetype may take the form of an anthropomorphic rendition of a force in Nature. Its potency derives from the fact that the observation of the sun's movement constitutes one of the universal, fundamental experiences of existence, and is something which man cannot change, a power beyond man's manipulation. The sun becomes an object of veneration, and magically one of a number of archetypes with which to identify in the ritual act of transcendence. Naturally different cultures would conceive of the sun-hero in a different form (e.g. Apollo-Helios in Greece, Ohrmazd in Ancient Persia) because traditions and styles colour the way we visualise things, but Jung regarded all of these as patterns on a theme. The core common to all of these representations being, in this instance the archetypal sun-god himself. But apart from its universality there was another side to the archetype; its vibrancy and to some extent its autonomy, or ability to appear separate.[23]

Jung adds: 'the "primordial images" or archetypes, lead their own independent life . . . as can easily be seen in those philosophical or gnostic systems which rely on awareness of the unconscious as the source of knowledge. The idea of angels, archangels, "principalities and powers" in St. Paul, the archons of the Gnostics, the heavenly hierarchy of Dionysius the Areopagite, all come from the perception of the relative *autonomy* of the archetypes.[24] Furthermore, an archetype contains within it a certain type of power or influence, and "it seizes hold of the psyche with a kind of primeval force".'[25]

From an analysis of his patients' dreams, Jung concluded that the vision of archetypes could cause delusions of grandeur and, to some extent, loss of free will. This interested him because he

---

[23] Elsewhere Jung wrote: 'The act of autonomy is such that psychologically, the spirit manifests itself as a *personal being, sometimes with visionary clarity* . . . in its strongest and most immediate manifestations it displays a peculiar life of its own which is felt as an independent being. . . .' ('Spirit and Life', 1926).
[24] C. G. Jung: '*Two Essays on Analytical Psychology*'. pp. 65–6.
[25] Ibid., p. 70.

came to see correlations between his patients and those visionaries who have shaped religious, mystical and magical belief as a result of their 'inner revelations'.

This connection is highly significant because, as will be indicated later, an integral part of High Magic is the stress on the Will of the individual. He has a choice of whether or not he will succumb to the primordial images brought into his range of vision through invocation. His ritual implements and symbolic actions help to reinforce the sense of identity so that in the enlargement of consciousness, the magician still retains control, despite the overwhelming force of the numinous imagery which he encounters.

One essential difference between a dream and a magical vision is that normally the former is undisciplined and unpredictable. The ritually inspired vision however is both induced and controlled, in the sense that one archetype rather than another is called forth and integrated.

Karl Kerenyi, a colleague of Jung's, has alluded to the 'archetype of the Divine Maiden', epitomized in Greek Mythology by Persephone. Daughter of Zeus and Demeter, Persephone was picking flowers on the Nysian plain when suddenly she was overwhelmed by the beauty of a narcissus. At that moment the earth opened and Aidoneus (Hades) rushed forth in his horse-drawn chariot and snatched her down into the bowels of the earth. Persephone called for her Father to help, but at first only Hecate, goddess of the Moon, and Helios the Sun god, could hear her pleas. Eventually Demeter, her Mother and goddess of fertility and the cereal crop, discovered the tragedy and sat in mourning causing the harvest to fail. Zeus sent Hermes to the Underworld to restore Persephone to life, but the latter, having eaten a pomegranate seed given to her by Hades, was now locked in endless transition between the world of the living and the dead. Kerenyi says in an essay on the Eleusinian mysteries that Demeter, the 'universal principal of life, and mother of the corn, and Persephone the ripened grain, are in a sense one and the same, for they symbolize the inextricable processes of cause and result, being and becoming'.[26] However Persephone is also the terrible Queen of the Underworld and has control over the powers governing death. In this dual aspect she thus embodies both death and rebirth, for the new crop appears cyclically as the old grain withers away.

From the viewpoint of Qabalistic magic this myth is highly significant for many reasons. Zeus and Demeter are the archetypal Father and Mother equating at the level of Demiurgos with Chokmah and Binah, the Supernal opposites. Their 'Son' Tiphareth, is the Helios of Greek mythology. Hecate, goddess of the Moon, and Persephone the divine Daughter of Zeus and Demeter, equate with the Sephiroth Yesod and Malkuth respectively. The importance of this is that as levels upon the Tree of Life, each of these archetypes represents a certain stage of consciousness, and resides beneath the Supernals as Helios/Tiphareth, Hecate/Yesod and Persephone/Malkuth on the Middle Pillar, the path of direct mystical 'ascent'.

In the myth itself, Hecate and Helios, the 'closest' archetypes to Persephone, are the first to know of her abduction. Only later does Demeter become aware of what has occurred. We see here that effects upon the consciousness are felt, in a sense, by 'reverberation' in the same way that Creation, in emanationist systems of mysticism, proceeds by degrees from one level to the next.

In modern ceremonial magic, Qabalistic mysticism has incorporated the Tarot to produce a practical system of exploring the recesses of the mind. Persephone, as an archetype, is the same as the female aspect[27] of the beautiful naked androgyne of 'The World', which symbolizes the 32nd Path linking Malkuth and Yesod, and constitutes the entrance to the lower levels of the unconscious. The magician, by medi-

---

[26] C. G. Jung and K. Kerenyi: *Essays on a Science of Mythology*. Harper and Row, New York, 1963, Section IV: 'Kore'.
[27] The male aspect, which arises because Malkuth reflects Kether, is Persephone's second husband Eubouleus who emerges from Hades with her, to lead a happy productive life.

tating upon the card and imaginatively visualizing it as a doorway, may proceed through it as the first step to higher levels of consciousness. The archetypal visions which he will encounter on the way are the anthropomorphic representations of the unconscious mind which, acting in a seemingly autonomous manner, profoundly modify the psyche as they come into view.

With reference to Jung's concept of archetypes, Jolande Jacobi writes: 'We find the archetypes recurring in all mythologies, fairy tales, religious traditions and mysteries. What are the myths of the 'night Sea journey', of the 'wandering hero' or of the sea monster, if not the eternal knowledge of the sun's setting and rebirth, transformed into images? Prometheus the Stealer of Fire, Heracles the dragon slayer, the countless creation myths, the fall from paradise, the mysteries of creation, the virgin birth, the treacherous betrayal of the hero, the dismembering of Osiris, and many other myths and fairy tales represent psychic processes in symbolic images. Similarly the figures of the snakes, the fish, the sphinx, the helpful animals, the Tree of the World, the Great Mother, the enchanted prince, the *puer aeternus*, the Mage, the Wise Man, Paradise, etc., stand for certain motifs and contents of the collective unconscious. In every single individual psyche they can awaken new life, exert their magic power and condense it into a kind of 'individual mythology'. . . . 'Thus for Jacobi and Jung the archetypes taken as a whole represent the sum of the latent potentialities of the human psyche—a vast store of ancestral knowledge about the profound relations between God, Man and Cosmos. . . .'[28]

In the Qabalah the archetypal Sephiroth align in three columns headed by the Supernals. The 'positive' column or pillar is headed by Chokmah the Father, representative of energy and force, provider of the life seed. Binah, the Great Mother, the receptive vehicle for the creative impulse, is his

[28] Jolande Jacobi: *The Psychology of C. G. Jung*. Routledge & Kegan Paul, London, 1968, p. 47.

polar opposite. The fusion of opposites occurs in the balanced Middle Pillar which in the highest reaches Kether, the Crown, the peak of Creation. On the same pillar, but at a level below Chokmah and Binah resides the fruit of their union, Tiphareth, the Son, symbol of resurrection, and spiritual rebirth. This constitutes the level of consciousness where man becomes god-like through sacrifice of his lower self.

It is interesting to note that the harmony of opposites as represented in the Tree of Life, was also axiomatic to Jung's understanding of psychoanalysis. We have referred earlier to the dream as compensating for unbalanced aspects of the personality, and it was this phenomenon which led Jung towards his idea of 'individuation', or *making the self whole*.

This is a key concept in all forms of mystical religion and High Magic, and it led Jung to analyse alchemy, which had been formerly regarded as a crude type of pre-chemistry, as a potential form of therapy. In this system man could be transformed into a complete being in harmony with, and not against, his unconscious.

Recently a very important illustration from the book *Pao P'u Tzu* by the fourth century Chinese alchemical writer Ko Hung has been alluded to by Kenneth Rexroth. The drawing shows a naked man meditating, with alchemical instruments (the retort, furnace and crucible, etc.) symbolically superimposed upon his body and corresponding to what Qabalists and students of Yoga call 'chakras', or 'spiritual centres'.[29]

This reinforces Jung's view that alchemy was in fact a form of integrative mysticism, and not merely a crude, randomly assembled collection of pseudo-scientific superstitions. Notwithstanding, Jung understood more about alchemy (he contributed a number of erudite volumes on the subject) than about the Qabalah or Rosicrucianism (which he superficially lumped with Theosophy and other modern movements as 'feeble substitutes' for Eleusis).

---

[29] Rexroth calls them 'major autonomic nervous system plexuses' in his introduction to Waite's *The Works of Thomas Vaughan*. University Book, New York, 1969.

His important contribution to the understanding of magic and religion lies in his exposition of the way in which the unconscious formulates such beliefs. For it is the unconscious spheres of the mind whose 'autonomous' forces impress us in dreams or inspire us as revelations in visions, and whose images man tends to worship as reflections of the divine.

Nevertheless, on one point, we must differ with Jung. Earlier, we referred to the so called 'out-of-the-body' experiences where the consciousness appears to operate separately from the physical organism. There are numerous medical cases of people finding themselves 'outside themselves', floating above their bodies and observing three-dimensional reality as if from a new vantage point. Such instances usually occur when the body is relaxed, and the individual is lying down (resting, about to go to sleep, etc.) although, as Celia Green points out, there are cases where the experience has occurred when the physical body is actively performing some function, and the 'consciousness component' observes it doing so.

Such cases of dual consciousness gave Jung, in particular, a great deal of trouble. They were clearly neither dream states nor states of normal consciousness, and thus defied classification within the unconscious/conscious categories. Jung and his colleague, Dr. Aniela Jaffe attempted to explain them by asserting that the unconscious was 'not merely "unconscious" or figuratively speaking, "dark", but (seemed) to be interspersed with spots of "brightness", of a quasi-consciousness . . . .'[30] These 'brightnesses' in the unconscious were referred to as 'luminosities' and were said to cluster, to form something like 'perceptive organs' in the unconscious.

This however is really nothing other than an elaborate way of saying that under certain circumstances the unconscious mind acts as if it is conscious. It might be easier to visualise consciousness as an activating principle which is normally

[30] Quoted from Robert Crookall: *The Jung-Jaffe View of Out-of-the-Body Experiences*. W.F.P. Plymouth, 1970, p. 16.

contingent to the physical organism but which, under certain conditions, may be removed from it.

Here anthropology is able to offer some additional assistance, in the area dealing with shamanism. Mircea Eliade has defined shamanism as a 'technique of ecstasy', the shaman being a magician who voluntarily 'specializes in a trance during which his soul is believed to leave his body and ascends to the sky, or descends to the underworld'. A parallel immediately arises between data collected recently by the Oxford Institute of Psychophysical Research under Celia Green, and the ethnographic material available on shamans in general.

The Iglulik Eskimos practice an initiation ceremony whereby the master 'extracts the disciple's "soul" from his eyes, brain and intestines, so that the spirits may know what is best in him. . . .' Enlightenment ('angakoq') follows, for the angakoq consists of 'a mysterious light which the shaman suddenly feels in his body, inside his head, within the brain, an inexplicable searchlight, a luminous fire, which enables him to see in the dark, both literally and metaphorically speaking, for he can now, even with closed eyes see through darkness, and perceive things which are hidden from others. . . .'[31]

The following case researched by the Oxford Institute is one where the person concerned induced an out-of-the-body experience using relaxation techniques.

> 'Each night in bed, lying on my back, I relaxed my body piece by piece, starting from the toes until, finally reaching the eyes, one was supposed to concentrate on an imaginary void between the eyebrows, then, filling it with a flower image, allow this to develop into full flower.
>
> 'For weeks I simply fell asleep at waist level, as it were, and gradually the idea of leaving the physical body became neglected, although the ritual of relaxing had become a habit.
>
> 'Then one night in the drowsy state before sleep I was aware of a small sensation which might be likened to a tablet of soap slipping from one's grasp in the bath. I was awake . . . I turned to

[31] Mircea Eliade: *Shamanism: Archaic Techniques of Ecstasy*. Routledge & Kegan Paul, London, 1964, p. 60.

look at my husband and was vaguely surprised to find that I was looking down at him and as I looked I rose higher and saw my sleeping form next to his.'[32]

Another case refers to seeing in the dark:

... 'There were heavy curtains at the window, so that the room was completely dark when they were drawn.

'In the middle of the night, I could suddenly see everything in the room in outline, as though there were a night light burning. I was very puzzled by this, and suddenly looked down, and saw myself lying in bed. I suppose I must have been three to four feet above the bed. . . .

'I seemed to panic . . . and decided that I should not be up there but down in the bed. . . .

'Going back into my body, gave me a kind of physical shock which woke me up, and I was very conscious of opening my eyes, although previously I had been able to see round the room, but now the room was black, and I could not see a thing. . . .'[33]

It is clear that a shaman is performing essentially the same feat when he leaves his body, as these instances described above. However, the shaman also employs the 'ecsomatic' experience for visionary purposes. He uses his 'alter ego' to travel into his 'unconscious' whereby he encounters the archetypal images as anthropomorphic forms. The profound insight arising from interaction with these forms constitutes his initiation.

An Avam Samoyed who wished to be a shaman was told that he would receive his 'gift' from the Lords of the Water. The neophyte was sick from smallpox at the time and 'the sickness troubled the water of the sea. The candidate came out and climbed a mountain. There he met a naked woman and began to suckle at her breast.' She said he was her child, and introduced him to her husband, the Lord of the Underworld, who gave him two animal guides, an ermine and a mouse, to escort him in the subterranean region. There he encountered the inhabitants of the underworld, the evil shamans, and the lords of epidemics, who instructed him in the nature of the diseases

[32] Celia Green: *Out-of-the-Body Experiences*. Institute of Psychophysical Research, Oxford, 1968, pp. 58–9.
[33] Celia Green: Op. cit., pp. 76–7.

plaguing mankind. Having had his heart ritually torn out and thrown into a pot, the candidate now travelled to the land of shamanesses where his throat and voice were strengthened, and then on to an island where the Tree of the Lord of the Earth rose up to the sky. The Lord gave him certain powers, among them the ability to cure the sick ('I am the Tree that gives life to all men'). Further he went, encountering magical stones that could speak, women covered with hair like a reindeer's, and a naked blacksmith, working a bellows over a huge fire in the bowels of the earth. Again the novice was ritually slain, and boiled over the fire in a cauldron for 'three years'. The blacksmith then forged the candidate's head on one of three anvils ('the one on which the best shamans were forged') and told him how to 'read inside his head', how to see mystically without his normal eyes, and how to understand the language of plants.

Having mastered these secrets, and having had his body constituted anew after immolation, the shaman awoke 'resurrected', as a revivified being.[34] He had encountered the archetypes with all their terrifying power, and emerged *knowledgeable*.

Such shamanistic experiences are recorded in many parts of the world. The Akawaio Carib shaman of British Guiana flies into the skies in his 'spirit form' with the assistance of a 'clairvoyant woman' disguised as a swallow-tailed kite. The Kalahari works himself into a trance in which the 'spirit' is said to 'boil up' and travel to the head, before leaving the body. Similarly, the Buryat shaman soars to the heavens and in his vision meets the gods of the Centre of the World and also his celestial 'wife', with whom he has sexual relations.

The Yaqui sorcerer Don Juan told his American 'chela' Carlos Castaneda that he should transform his consciousness into that of a crow if he wished to 'fly' from his body. On another occasion, Castaneda was meditating on a stream of water which he wanted to use as a vehicle for 'travelling'. Don

[34] Mircea Eliade: Op. cit., p. 40.

Juan warned that he should not allow his consciousness to be swept too far away. ('Look at the water in front of you,' I heard him saying, 'but don't let its sound carry you anywhere. If you let the sound of the water carry you I may never be able to find you and bring you back.')[35]

The Vasyugan shaman likewise cultivated a 'spirit of the head', that is to say, an image to which he could transfer consciousness. In the form of a bear he would travel to the underworld, and upon a grey horse he would ride into the sky.

Other creatures popular among shamans for such purposes include the wolf, reindeer, tiger and fish.

From such documentation it becomes evident that there exists a means whereby a person may extricate his consciousness from his physical body and allow it either to observe three-dimensional reality from a different vantage point (e.g. near the ceiling, up in the air), or to enter *consciously* into a vision deriving from the inner regions of the unconscious. In the latter case the visionary will encounter, as if they were real, archetypal images in the form of gods and goddesses sheathed in the colours and styles of his own culture. Thus the Eleusian neophyte experiences a vision of the cereal goddess Demeter, the Samoyed shaman meets strange nature deities under the earth, and the Yaqui sorcerer meets his peyote deity, Mescalito, in the fields.

In the West, the aim of the Qabalistic magician is to integrate the archetypes which form a sequence leading up to and culminating in, Tiphareth. These include Malkuth (Persephone) the Divine Maiden; Yesod (Hecate) the region of the white goddess of the Moon; Hod (Hermes) the messenger of the Creative Intelligence; and Netzach (Aphrodite) the goddess of Love and Nature. The integration of Tiphareth, which is in itself the centre of the Tree of Life, constitutes a new order of being far above the level of normal consciousness.

We have so far considered various academic attitudes to religious and magical beliefs. Leaving aside the question of

[35] Carlos Castaneda: *A Separate Reality*. The Bodley Head, London, 1971, p. 208.

origins, it may indeed be possible to establish social patterns demonstrating the way in which human beings formulate beliefs. Thus when an Australian aboriginee refers to Bungurdi, the Kangaroo totem and Being of the Dawn-Time, as his 'kadja' or brother, it may be a possibility that the belief similarly unites all his clansmen as 'brothers', thus strengthening society, or again we can point to the existence of patterns in mythology and dreams which as archetypes manifest universally, irrespective of the culture concerned. But one question remains to be asked. *Who* is it that believes? Obviously regardless of context or child development, it is the individual. My belief about a totem being (or any being) may ostensibly be the same as yours, but I can only be sure of my own perception of the belief, for this perception is my own experience and ultimately, only my own. Your belief is similarly unique and focused centrally in your own individuality alone. The movement which drew attention to this important point was of course existentialism, popular in Europe since World War II, and still a potent factor in contemporary thought.

Existentialism draws a primary distinction between essence and existence. When we speak of essence, says the existentialist, we refer to categories that differentiate one thing from another, in a sense similar to Plato's concept of Forms which explains the single reality behind appearance in its numerous manifestations. Each man's view of a particular thing differs, although the essence of the thing remains the same, consequently each individual's judgment of a particular thing or event will be differently coloured.

This has led to an insistence by Jean-Paul Sartre, among others, that a man moves solely within his *own* universe, he has a free choice as to how he will act, and his actions are his responsibility alone. There are no 'norms' or 'universals' for judging such behaviour, no code of 'good and evil'. There are only observable actions. Neither are there any scapegoats upon whom a man can unload his responsibility, for he is 'condemned to be free', and to endure his own isolation. In addition, says

Sartre, freedom is a characteristic of humans because they can make a choice which affects their very being. Therefore man is not only isolated from other men, but from the whole of non-thinking creation. Sartre uses as an example Pierre's room. Pierre, says Sartre remains separate from his room because of the mode of his existence. The room, with its books, table and papers, remains the same whether Pierre is there or not. These sundry objects exist as themselves only, Pierre however can change because by making decisions about the direction in which his life shall tend, he becomes a new being by degrees. His is forever transcending his old self.

To return to the original point, he is the only one who can *experience* this change, others may hear about aspects of his life, actions and behaviour, but then their experience hinges on the way in which they themselves perceive Pierre.

Sartre's world-view is a pessimistic one, because it excludes purpose and meaning from existence, and it is not shared by all existentialists although his name has become to some extent synonymous with the term. Soren Kierkegaard and Gabriel Marcel both postulated a universe which admitted the Being of God, and since God was responsible for man's existence, the relationship between man and God needed to be developed; therein lay meaning and hope. Martin Buber, the Jewish philosopher and theologian similarly rejected Sartre's solitary universe in advocating that such a view entailed denuding the Cosmos of dignity. The 'I-Thou' relationship between man and the Eternal could never be reduced merely to 'I-It'. Sartre was making the *self* the only worthwhile focus. In *Eclipse of God* Buber wrote: 'selfhood ... has become omnipotent (and) with all the 'It' around it, can naturally acknowledge neither God, nor any genuine Absolute which manifests itself to men as of non-human origin.'

Emmanuel Mounier, a friend of Sartre's, also rejected the latter's isolationism. Referring to himself as a Personalist rather than as an Existentialist, Mounier maintained that the individual was unique within nature for his capacity to form relationships with other people. Communication of love or the desire to share knowledge was what bonded people together and lifted them from their solitariness.

In summary we can say that, even taking these extra considerations into account, it remains basic that experience as such is individually orientated. Whether I see myself as the *only* reality is a matter of choice. Extending this, we may say that even if belief in Gods and demons is shaped by unconscious forms and forces, and by the nature of social custom, in the final assessment it is only meaningful to talk of *one person's* belief or vision as opposed to another's.

However, it is obviously crucial to consider the possible sources of inspiration for these beliefs, for in certain important instances they have derived from visionary experiences at a profoundly high level of consciousness.

CHAPTER TWO

Avatars and Gnostikoi

We need to consider that form of mysticism which finally unites religion and magic, both reflecting the effort of man to become whole and to become one with the logos of the Universe.

William James has written in his penetrating lectures on religion that 'personal religious experience has its root and centre in mystical states of consciousness.' It is through a heightening of consciousness that man transcends himself and it is on this basis that the materialistic aspect of existentialism reveals its limitations, for under these new conditions man becomes greater than man, and the Godhead surges through him so that his whole universe becomes limitless. Mystical experiences . . . are 'states of knowledge', wrote James, . . . 'They are illuminations, revelations full of significance and importance . . . the mystic feels as if his own will were in abeyance and indeed sometimes as if he were grasped and held by a superior power.'

The men who have had such experiences are those who shape religions, who found mystical orders as a result of their vision, and who guide or tutor those who have not had such insights so that they might obtain them. Such men are the avatars[36] of religion and the initiates of High Magic, those who bring back from the heights of consciousness an expression of Reality.

---

[36] An avatar is a human being who incarnates God. Christianity holds that there has been only one, Jesus Christ, although Hinduism and Buddhism concede that there have been many.

AVATARS AND GNOSTIKOI

In the *Bhagavad-Gita* the words of the Eternal logos are written: 'When goodness grows weak, when evil increases, I make myself a body. In every age I come back, To deliver the holy....'

Through the ages there have been men whose heightened awareness have enabled them to speak with authority of the Divine, and of man's relationship with it: of man's evolutionary direction and the laws of his existence. Amongst these men, Zarathustra, Mohammed, Moses and Christ have probably contributed more to shaping the Western consciousness than any other avatars.

Zarathustra, the greatest of the thirteen religious teachers and reformers to bear the Zoroastrian title, was born probably around 570 B.C., and inherited the Persian tendency towards dualism in which the cosmic principles of good and evil were locked in eternal conflict. Nevertheless he seems as Bouquet has said, to have taken the role, like Mohammed, of endeavouring 'to recall his people to a purer faith', and he introduces a notable element of monotheism.

In the *Gathas*, which are a collection of songs, oracles, and hymns, allegedly written by Zarathustra himself, Ahura-Mazda, who already existed as a concept in Persia prior to the prophet's birth,[37] is modified so he is seen as essentially *one Being* with ambivalent qualities. He is thus 'Creator of all things through the Holy Spirit', and 'Creator of good thought'. However, he is also Father of Light and Darkness, Good and Evil, Life and not-Life, which were personified respectively as Spenta Mainyu and Angra Mainyu, the opposing twins. He is the *one Reality* behind duality. In later Zoroastrianism Ahura-Mazda as Ohrmazd becomes specifically identified with light and goodness, in conflict with Ahriman who represents evil and darkness, but even here Ohrmazd is held to be finally victorious. Zarathustra thus remoulded the essential dualism in allowing the principle of light the ultimate triumph.

[37] Zaehner has put forward the hypothesis that Ahura-Mazda may be a derivative of the Indian Sky god Varuna, of the Rig Veda.

It is possible that in so doing, Zarathustra was harkening back to a principle of one-ness which may have actually long preceded the characteristic duality of Persian religion. As Brandon points out, such one-ness was by no means atypical: Mithra was worshipped in both eastern and western Persia as a sky god incorporating both light and dark, day and night. Vayu was a wind god with both good and bad qualities, and Zurvan the god of infinite Time, was regarded well before the fourth century B.C. as the originator of both good and evil.

Mithraism was later brought to Italy as a result of the expeditions of Trajan, Lucius Verus and Septimius Severus and became an active force in Rome and the Empire at large, by the end of the first century A.D. Zurvan (also called Aeon, Aion or Kronos) penetrated the Occident as an aspect of Mithra, combining human and lion-like characteristics with his body enveloped by a coiled serpent representing the Universe, and Lord of the Zodiac and Seasons, he united in his own being 'the power of all the gods, whom he alone (had) begotten'.[38]

Especially interesting in light of the Gnostics' claim that they held the secret interpretation to many of Christ's teachings, is the fact that the Basilidean deity Abraxas seems to have derived partly from Mithra/Zurvan. Both Abraxas and the Persian deity were high-gods encompassing opposite polarities and the numerical value of both names totalled 365, as Budge has shown,[39] this being the number of days in a year, the unit of cyclic time. Both Abraxas and Mithra in his Zurvan-Time aspect ruled over eternity, the cycles of time being measured by the path of the Sun, and in the same way that this was symbolised in Zurvan by means of a coiled snake, Abraxas was similarly represented with serpentine coils instead of legs.

---

[38] Franz Cumont: *The Mysteries of Mithra*. Dover Publications Inc., New York, 1956, p. 109.

[39] Budge gives the following annotation in his work *Amulets and Talismans* (University Books, New York 1961) p. 208. *Abraxas*: A = 1, B = 2, P = 100, A = 1, [= 200; A = 1 and Ƶ = 60. Total 365. *Mithras*: M = 40, E = 5, I = 10, Θ = 9, P = 100, A = 1, and [= 200. Total 365.

AVATARS AND GNOSTIKOI

But we shall consider the Gnostic relationship to Christianity presently.

In the same way that Zarathustra had endeavoured to modify the dualism of his contemporaries, Mohammed similarly felt that his main mission was to purify the religious climate in which he found himself. The Arab nation was quite heterodox in this respect. At the time of Mohammed's birth in A.D. 570 there had already been Jewish and Magian incursions, and even some Christian converts including in their number Al Nooman Abu Kabus, King of Hira, and his grandfather Mondar. A sect calling themselves Collyridians[40] worshipped the Virgin Mary as God, and it was also believed in some heretical circles that the soul died with the body and was raised again on the Last Day. Mohammed, though, was to find his greatest opponent in the Sabian religion which was monotheistic in theory, but also involved in practice, the worship of the fixed stars, angels and other intermediary intelligences in addition to the one God who resided over them. Their observances included lengthy sessions of prayer and fasting, and also sacrifices of food. Among their holy books were the biblical Psalms and a Chaldean moralistic tome entitled the Book of Seth. The Sabians held the pyramids of Egypt in awe as the sepulchres of Seth, Enoch, Sabi, and his two sons, the latter providing the name of their religion.[41]

In particular, Mohammed objected to the way in which the Sabians worshipped stone figurines and set as one of his main aims, the purging of idolatory in all its forms. In its place would stand the worship of the one God, Al Ilah, or Allah.

Mohammed had heard supernatural voices, while walking in the desert near Mecca, which told him that he was Allah's chosen prophet. Finally when he was forty he had a vision of the archangel Gabriel in a lonely cave, wherein he was shown a silken cloth on which were inscribed the following words:

---

[40] From the word 'collyris' denoting a cake offered to the Virgin.
[41] It is also possible that the name 'Sabian' derives from 'Saba' meaning 'the host of Heaven'.

'Thy Lord . . . hath created all things . . . (and) hath created man of congealed blood[42] . . . Verily, man becometh insolent because he seeth himself abound in riches. Verily unto thy Lord shall be the return of all'[43]

On another occasion he was solemnly warned that man must 'avoid speaking that which is false, being orthodox in respect of God, associating no other God with Him. . . .' But in this Sura lay the instruction which was to unleash a creed of violence:

> 'Permission is granted unto those who take arms against the unbeliever. . . . And if God did not repel the violence of some men by others, verily monasteries and churches and synagogues and the temples of the Moslems, wherein the name of God is frequently commemorated, they would be utterly demolished. And God will certainly assist him who shall be on His side, for God is strong and mighty. . . .'[44]

While in Medina, it occurred to Mohammed that especially because man's future life lay at stake, it would be necessary for him as Allah's appointed Prophet, to subdue by force both Arabia and ultimately the whole world. There were after all only two alternatives, paradise or eternal damnation:

> . . . '*they who believe not* shall have garments of fire fitted unto them, boiling water shall be poured on their heads; their bowels shall be dissolved thereby, and also their skins; and they shall be beaten with maces of iron. So often as they shall endeavour to get out of Hell, because of the anguish of their torments, they shall be dragged back into the same: and their tormentors shall say unto them, 'Taste ye the pain of burning'.

> 'God will introduce *those who shall believe and act righteously* into gardens through which rivers flow, they shall be adorned therein with bracelets of gold and pearls,[45] and their vestures therein shall be silk. . . .'

---

[42] With the exception of Adam, Eve, and Jesus.
[43] Sura 96 (Koran).
[44] Sura 22 (Koran).
[45] A rather ironic promise in the light of man's faults. See Sura 96 (Koran).

AVATARS AND GNOSTIKOI

Mohammed engaged in twenty-seven battles within his own country to extend the fruits of his vision by the sword. In the year A.D. 630 he also placed three thousand men in the field against one hundred thousand Greeks in order to avenge the death of an ambassador sent to Bosra who, unknown to Mohammed, had actually been slain by an Arab. After an early setback Mohammed's general Khâled Ebn al Walid was able to win the day. In the same year, Mohammed took Mecca.

The Koran[46] teaches the unity of Allah and asserts that there can never be more than one true religion, hence Mohammed's intolerance. God is not liable to change in Himself (although his will was often unintelligible and apparently arbitrary in man's eyes). Prophets have been sent to prevent mankind from erring from the true and desirable way. Two early prophets included Hûd, whose unbelieving audience Allah punished with a hot, suffocating wind, and Sâleh, who once caused a she-camel to manifest from a rock.

Mohammed divided Islam (which means 'submission') into 'Iman' (faith) and 'Din' (practices, prayer, alms, fasting and the pilgrimage to Mecca). His doctrine, which is of most interest to us here, entailed six sub-sections. Belief in God, his angels, his scriptures, his prophets, the Resurrection and Day of Judgement, and God's control of good and evil.'[47] There are four main angels in Islam, and they have bodies of fire. Gabriel, the Holy Spirit, angel of revelations and divine decrees, Michael, protector of the Jews; Azrael, angel of death; and Israfil, who blows the trumpet at the Resurrection. George Sale, whose translation and notes we are deeply indebted to, makes the interesting observation that these four archangels parallel 'almost in the same manner . . . the apocryphal gospel of Barnabus, where it is said that Gabriel reveals the secrets of

---

[46] Mohammed actually wrote the Koran, although some Moslems assert that the original is in Heaven and that it was delivered to Mohammed by Gabriel in bundles bound in silk and embossed with precious stones from Paradise, over a space of twenty-three years.

[47] Due to God's 'arbitrary' Will, good and evil could not be regarded as absolutes.

APPROACHES

God, Michael combats against his enemies, Raphael receives the souls of those who die, and Uriel is to call everyone to judgement on the last day'. The same archangels also represent the Four Elements in the Jewish Qabalah, Raphael, Air; Gabriel, Water; Michael, Fire; and Uriel, Earth.

The Devil, Eblis, also features in the Koran as an angel who was once close to God, but who fell from grace for disobeying a command. Other than these main supernatural beings in the sacred texts are the Djin or Genii, fire creatures subject to death unlike archangels, and capable of both good and evil. On a human level, every man was believed to be continually under the auspices of two angels who noted his actions, which in turn determined his fate.

Moses and Jesus were said to be the most important harbingers of truth other than Mohammed himself, who was held to be the final, and most illustrious of the prophets.

Prior to Mohammed in about 1900 B.C., Abram, a refugee from the destruction of Ur caused by the Elamite hordes, meditated on another form of monotheism. Abram's monotheism was unlike that of contemporary religions which incorporated a pantheon which was an expression of one high-god: Abram saw his God as a Creator independent of any natural or geographical limitations, whose preoccupation with justice and righteousness was of paramount importance. Abram's revelation and Covenant with his god in Canaan formed the basis of the Hebrew religion. In Genesis 15.7 and 17.4 this Covenant is expressed as 'I am YHVH that brought thee out of Ur of the Chaldees, to give thee this land to inherit . . . my Covenant is with thee, and thou shalt be a father of many nations. Neither shall thy name any more be called Abram, but thy name shall be Abraham'. This change of name is significant, in that Abraham literally means 'Father of a great multitude', signifying according to Isidore Epstein, that the Covenant embraced all the familes of the earth.

This pattern of God renaming his chosen is continued in later generations, where for example, Jacob was renamed

AVATARS AND GNOSTIKOI

Israel ('the champion of God'), after a mystical experience in which he wrestled with an angel, whilst trying to storm Heaven by the ladder provided for angels to travel to and from the Earth.

During the reign of Thothmes (1485–1450 B.C.) when the Hebrew tribes were subjected to severe oppression, Moses[48] was brought up as the adopted son of an Egyptian princess (probably Hatshepsut) and lived as an Egyptian noble, learning the arts and sciences of Egypt. In fact, Josephus gives an account of a successful expedition which Moses conducted on behalf of the king of Egypt against the Ethiopians, who had invaded Egypt as far north as Memphis. However, he fell foul of the authorities by killing an Egyptian who was chastising a Hebrew slave, and had to flee the country for the grazing lands of Midian.

After spending 'forty years' as a shepherd in the wilderness, he was shown a vision of a flaming bush near Mt. Horeb, from which a voice proceeded identifying itself as 'the God of the Fathers, the God of Abraham, Isaac, and Jacob', EHYH ASHR EHYH, a form which differed from the name YHVH which was given to Abraham. Moses resisted the call till the 'anger of the Lord was kindled against him', but finally left for Egypt where he arrived shortly after the beginning of the reign of Amenhotep (1450–1421 B.C.) who had instituted quite ruthless measures against the Hebrew slaves.

Before Moses could achieve the liberation of the Hebrew people, it was necessary for him to convince both his people that the God whose dispensation he brought was the God of their Fathers, and to convince Amenhotep that he had the necessary power to enforce his demands. This was accomplished by the medium of a series of natural phenomenon known as the Ten Plagues.[49] Eventually the Hebrew tribes were allowed to

---
[48] The Egyptian name of Moses, according to Manetho, and quoted by Philo, was Osarsiph. Osarsiph was attached to the school of the Great Temple of Heliopolis.
[49] A show of magical strength against the Egyptian magicians.

leave Egypt, together with a number of slaves of other nationalities.[50]

After a series of incidents they reached Mt. Sinai where Moses again made Israel's Covenant with God, a Covenant which had its roots in Abraham's Covenant, and even earlier in the Covenant of Noah. It is this Covenant, incorporating as it does the Decalogue, the civil and religious code of Jews, and the details of their ark and later temples, which has welded the beliefs of the tribes of Israel into one of the world's most enduring religions and preserved its monotheistic integrity for almost four millennia. This Covenant also established Moses as the lawgiver of the Hebrew people.

Although the worship of YHVH suffered many vicissitudes between the time when the Hebrew people settled in Canaan in the fourteenth century B.C. and the beginning of the Christian Era, the code of ethics and behaviour incorporated in the Pentateuch (the first five books of the Bible) helped Israel's monotheism to survive the incursions of local Baals and Astartes. As a result of lapses in favour of other gods a series of 'Judges', Prophets and Priests continued to remind 'God's chosen people' that YHVH was a jealous God and would not tolerate being included among the local pantheons. This succession climaxed in the welding together of the Hebrew people under David and his successor, Solomon (*circa* 1012–931 B.C.), a period which constituted the Golden Era of the Hebrew people.

It was the revolt of Jeroboam (*circa* 931 B.C.) which destroyed the kingdom of Israel and split the original twelve tribes into the province of Judah (including the tribe of Benjamin which remained loyal to the House of David) and the other ten tribes, the Kingdom of Israel. These two states, caught between the great powers of Assyria and Egypt, paid alternate tribute to one and then the other until 721 B.C. when Israel fell to Sargon II,

[50] The Pharaoh Merenptah (reigned *circa* 1227–1218 B.C.) whom Moses defied had an obelisk erected later, to commemorate his *driving out* of Egypt the foreigners of the delta area.

and 586 B.C. when Judah (with its capital Jerusalem) fell to Nebuchadnezzar. The Hebrew people finally dispersed among a multitude of nations after the Roman sacking of Jerusalem in A.D. 70 and they remained so until the re-creation of the state of Israel in 1948. And despite the Diaspora, the Hebrew people have retained their culture, religion, code of ethics and life style.

The keystone of this resilience has been the Torah, the written laws of the Pentateuch, its commentaries the Midrashim, the oral tradition of the Mishnah, and the works of Prophets, Psalmists, and Chroniclers which made up the bulk of the Old Testament. Because there has been a religious awe of the written word throughout the history of the Hebrew people, the corpus of Hebrew writings has probably been less tampered with than any other body of religious documents, so that the Laws of Moses have survived to have an enduring effect upon both the Jews and Christians of the Western world. In fact, according to the Mishnah there existed early in the history of Israel a copy of the Pentateuch kept in the Temple (called 'The Scroll of the Temple Court' or the 'Scroll of Ezra') which provided an ultimate reference for the correction of privately owned copies. Another example of the almost fanatical preservation of the *letter* of the Law came to light during the last century when a large collection of manuscript and book fragments was discovered in the Ezra Synagogue in Cairo where they had been deposited (rather than discarded) because of the sanctity ascribed to all such texts.

Another injunction which has been an important factor in keeping the Hebrew people together, despite their lack of a common home, has been the laws forbidding intermarriage with the people of other religions and cultures. This injunction, together with the common bond of the Torah has maintained the integrity of the Jewish religion to a far greater extent than the integrity which existed whilst they dwelt in Canaan.

The final establishment of the contents of the written Torah, together with the editing of the Midrashim and transcription of the Mishnah, occurred under the auspices of Rabbi Jochanan ben Zakkai and the Jabneh Sanhedrin during the first century of the Christian era. For the next two thousand years most Jewish religious and mystical works have been commentaries on, or based on texts from, the Pentateuch of Moses established at Jabneh. Such works as the Talmud (which includes the Mishnah together with the Gemara) and the Zohar, although the latter uses texts from the Pentateuch more as an introduction to its theme rather than a passage for exegesis, have been built around this Pentateuch.

After the revolt of the Jews who were under Hadrian's rule (in A.D. 135), the Jewish people were repressed to the point where the death penalty was awarded for any who studied the Torah. To escape this repression they migrated to the four corners of the earth, preserving their national consciousness through a literary rather than a geographical bond. Those Jews who professed Christianity (which had till then been regarded as an offshoot sect of Judaism) were unable to embrace the concept of a nation divorced from its territory, and so, under threat of persecution, ceased the practice of many of the precepts of Judaism, and combined with the converts from the surrounding religions who had been attracted to Christianity through the proselytizing of Paul.

At this time, in fact, the Near East was inundated with competing traditions; the Hellenistic mysteries, the religions of Mithra and Osiris, and the Chaldean astrological cults, among others, and all this primarily as a result of the earlier Alexandrian conquests and the ensuing interchange between East and West. Samuel Angus writes: 'Where men of every degree of culture, of every civilised race and representative of every ancient religion met together under the rule of one man (Alexander) there was ample room for the interchange of thought.'[51] This interchange was hastened by the rapid growth of trade routes, along which were carried not only commercial wares but also Near-Eastern and oriental mystical ideas. It is

---

[51] Samuel Angus: *The Mystery Religions and Christianity*. University Books, New York 1966, p. 157.

AVATARS AND GNOSTIKOI

therefore not surprising to find parallels between the legends surrounding the great religious figures.

Kenneth Walker has indicated certain similarities between Christ and Buddha for example:[52] both were born of a virgin, both were offered worldly power by the Devil, both cured the lame and blind, both had followers who tried to walk on the water but who sank due to lack of faith. There are other points of comparison as well; both had twelve followers, and both fed a large crowd with a small portion of food. This tends to support Jung's view that great men become imbued with an archetypal superhuman aura and legendary powers. However, it does not lessen the value of their specific teachings, for, as Walker says: 'If it be true that, in its early formative stage, Christianity derived help from the older established Buddhism, there is nothing that need distress Christians in that idea. Whether historically connected or not, Christianity and Buddhism were twin expressions of one great spiritual movement. The existence of similarities, far from discrediting either religion, reveals the unity of religious feeling, a unity that is so complete that even the words and parables used by the great teachers are often the same.'[53]

What is perhaps even more interesting is that both Buddhism and Christianity had, and Buddhism still has, a hidden side to its teaching which was not given out publicly, but only to those who were capable of receiving it.

In Buddhism, the division between the Hinayana and Mahayana systems derives from a council of Buddhists at Patna during the reign of Asoka which split into the orthodox Vibhajjauadius (eventually the Southern or Hinayana Buddhists) and the orthodox Sarvastivadins (eventually the Northern or Mahayana Buddhists). It has been suggested that the Mahayana doctrine is the teaching of Buddha as given to the Elect and that the Hinayana (also called Theraveda) system constitutes his more pragmatic 'outer' teaching.

---
[52] Kenneth Walker: *Diagnosis of Man*, Pelican Books, 1962.
[53] Kenneth Walker: Ibid., p. 214.

APPROACHES

Heinrich Zimmer writes: 'It is said by some, that when the Buddha began teaching his doctrine, he soon realised that men were not prepared to accept it in its fullness. They shrank from the extreme implications of his vision of the universal Void (Sunyata). Therefore he committed the deeper interpretation of reality to an audience of Nagas (serpents) who were to hold it in trust until mankind should be made ready to understand. Then to his human disciples he offered, as a kind of preliminary training and approach to the paradoxical truth, the comparatively rational and realistic doctrine of the so-called Hinayana division of Buddhism. Not until some seven centuries had passed was the great sage Nagarjuna, "Arjuna of the Nagas", initiated by the serpent kings into the truth that all is Void (Sunya). And so it was he who brought to man, the full-fledged Buddhist teachings of the Mahayana.'[54]

It is true that the doctrine of the Void is not followed by the Southern Buddhists in the complex form of the North, and the Mahayana Buddhists also place more emphasis on Bodhisattvas, beings who have achieved supreme insight into reality and who can assist mankind through their wisdom. In the North there is an elaborate system of divine emanations and a greater emphasis on Yoga as the pragmatic means to the experience of the Great Realization, than in the South where Yoga is more a theoretical study than a practice.[55] Northern Buddhism expounds an esoteric interpretation of the Trinity Tri-Kaya, whereas in the South there is more of a fundamentalist adherence to the text of the Pali Canon. In summary, the Mahayana Buddhists do not reject what the Hinayana advocates profess, they merely claim that it is incomplete, and capable of a more profound interpretation.

The same idea, of exoteric and esoteric levels of understanding, seems to be present in the words of Christ speaking to his

---

[54] Heinrich Zimmer: *Myths and Symbols in Indian Art and Civilization*: Harper and Row, 1962, p. 68.
[55] W. Y. Evans-Wentz: *The Tibetan Book of the Dead*. Oxford University Press, New York, 1960, p. 232.

disciples: 'Unto you it is given to know the mystery of the Kingdom of God: but unto them that are without, all these things are done in parables.'[56] Clement of Alexandria, the Church Father who lived towards the end of the second century A.D., similarly affirmed that Christ's teachings were two-fold; and were in part 'designed not for the multitude but communicated to those only who were capable of receiving them orally'. In his now-lost work '*The Institutions*' he writes: 'The Lord imparted the Gnosis to James the Just, to John and Peter after His resurrection; these delivered it to the rest of the Apostles, and they to the Seventy'[57] (i.e. the translators of the Hebrew scriptures). Joseph Head and S. L. Cranston ask: 'In the New Testament we have the parables, but what happened to the inner teaching?'[58]

The Gnostics have traditionally been regarded merely as heretical deviants from the true Christianity. However, it now seems that this view is incorrect. Not only was Gnosticism 'one of the most powerful currents of thought which influenced Christian doctrine and practice', as in Radhakrishnan's view, but it may be crucial to a study of Christian origins. In the introduction to his translation of the Gnostic Bruce Codex rendered into English as '*The Gnosis of the Light*', the Reverend A. A. F. Lamplugh writes: 'Recent investigations have challenged the traditional outlook and the traditional conclusions ... the burning question is, or will be—not how did a peculiarly silly and licentious heresy rise within the Church—but how did the Church rise out of the Great Gnostic movement. . . .'[59]

In Smith and Wace's '*Dictionary of Christian Biography*' it is stated:

'We have no reason to think that the earliest Gnostics intended to found sects separated from the Church and called after their

[56] Mark 4:11.
[57] This is reminiscent of the seventy Elders to whom Moses allegedly entrusted the doctrines of the Qabalah after his descent from Sinai.
[58] Their excellent book *Reincarnation in World Thought* contains some important Gnostic references pertinent to this question. See p. 108 *et seq.*
[59] *The Gnosis of the Light*, John Watkins, London, 1918.

own names. Their disciples were to be Christians, elevated above the rest as acquainted with deeper mysteries and called Gnostikoi, because possessed of a gnosis superior to the simple faith of the multitude'.[60]

We are reminded that one of the most important Gnostic teachers, Basilides, claimed his doctrines derived ultimately from the Apostles Matthew and Peter.[61] Included among the other major Gnostic sects, were the Ophites, Valentinians, Ebionites, and the Simonists, followers of Simon Magus. Of the surviving Gnostic documents a considerable number are of Hellenistic or Egyptian derivation, substantially outside Judaism. It is clear, however, that the very early Church Fathers welcomed the Gnostic-Hermetic tracts, although it eventually became clear to the builders of Church and dogma that, judging by these writings, Christ's life and teachings had extensive antecedents and could not be regarded as unique.[62] In the view of G. R. S. Mead, one of the foremost authorities on Gnosticism, it was for this reason that the Gnostic literature was later in wide measure proclaimed heretical and suppressed.

Although the Gnostic sects varied considerably there were certain features which the main groups had in common. Chief among these was the already referred to mystical principle of Sacred Emanations which probably originated in the East.

William Kingsland in his book *The Gnosis or Ancient Wisdom in the Christian Scripture* states: 'Most of the so-called Gnostic Schools or Sects were distinguished by an elaborate Cosmology

---

[60] See the article on Gnosticism, Vol. II, p. 679.

[61] Basilides was convinced that Christ had provided his apostles with a more enlightened dogma than that given to the masses. His 'Interpretations of the Gospels', however were burned by the church as heretical.

[62] This was an unpardonable conclusion. The Church was inclined to interpret Christ as the only Son of God and was unwilling to admit that any other avatars were or could be of equal stature. As Mircea Eliade has indicated, Western religion has a temporal emphasis with great importance being attached to the Final Judgement. Eastern religion on the other hand is more cyclic, and it was this characteristic which had crept into Gnostic Hermeticism. A cycle, with its implications of greater things to come in the future, would tend to lessen the 'once only' nature of the Christ which the Church wished to present, and would similarly undermine the intermediary authoritative capacity of the Church itself.

or Aeonology, the fundamental principle of which was a succession of emanations from the One of a series of Creative Powers in descending order, each having its appointed sphere of action in the economy of the Cosmos as a whole, from "Spirit" to "Matter". The names and functions of these Powers varied very considerably in different systems. . . .'[63]

The creation of the world as we know it was thus a gradual process, involving a hierarchy of secondary or intermediary Beings. Employing this framework, a number of Gnostic sects were quite explicit about the relationship of Christ to the Godhead, and the nature of these two entities. Mead writes: 'In pursuit of a universal ideal, the tribal God—or rather the crude views of the uninstructed Jewish populace as to Yahweh was, when not entirely rejected, placed in a very subordinate position. In brief, the Yahweh of the Elohim was not the Father of Jesus; the Demiurgos or creative power of the world, was not the Mystery God over all.'[64] In other words, the Spirit that created and shaped the world was not the First Principle, but only an intermediary power, an emanation far removed from the lofty heights of the Ultimate, unmanifest Godhead.

The person Jesus was usually regarded as being 'Christ, the divine Aeon or perfected man' incarnate in a human vehicle. 'God in Christ, did not suffer, but appeared to suffer; the lower man Jesus, alone suffered.'[65] In an unnamed tract which in many ways parallels the teachings of Basilides, the Ophites and the *Pistis Sophia*, and which is referred to by Irenaeus, Jesus incorporates both the Christos principle (logos) and also the feminine Sophia or Wisdom, his inspiration deriving from the Higher Spheres whose Light becomes part of his very being.[66]

This is more elaborately formulated in the important Gnostic

---

[63] William Kingsland: *The Gnosis or Ancient Wisdom in the Christian Scriptures.* George Allen and Unwin, London, 1937 p. 102.
[64] G. R. S. Mead: *Fragments of a Faith Forgotten.* University Books, New York, 1960, p. 138.
[65] G. R. S. Mead: Ibid., p. 141.
[66] See also our reference to the Ophite conception of Christ in *The Search for Abraxas,* Neville Spearman, London, 1970, Section I, II.

work the so-called *Bruce Codex*, named after its discoverer. Written in Coptic, this papyrus probably dates from the second or third century A.D. and has possible Egyptian or Greek antecedents. In this work Christ embodies the essence of the Pleroma or Perfect Nature, which was held by the Gnostics to be the most exalted realm of existence. In fact, from this level derived the only true Knowledge and it was this which Jesus allegedly passed on to his Apostles. Jesus says: 'Happy is the man . . . who has brought down Heaven unto Earth, who has taken the Earth and raised it to the Heavens, so that they are no longer divided.' Clearly Heaven, in this system, is a state of high consciousness, for Christ goes on to say 'If you know my Word you may make Heaven descend upon Earth *so that it may abide in you.*' The basis for all Being, says Christ, is the Supreme Monad 'which is unknowable and which no man hath known, that hath no Symbol (for) all Symbols are in it', the subsequent Pleroma and Aeon-deities, and the world itself all owe their existence to this One Principle. 'This is He, the True God, the Only Begotten, the All; the Aeons of the Pleroma know that it is by Him that they have become Gods and they have become holy in this Name.' Paralleling the Qabalah, the Monad has the same relationship to the Pleroma as the Great Unmanifest has to Kether, the Crown. 'The Pleroma adores Him for His Beauty and His Goodness; those who are in the Pleroma form His Crown; those who are without are under His Feet, and those who are in the midst thereof surround Him.'[67]

Gnosis, the fourth of Five Powers resident in the 'Incommensurate Abyss' (the other Powers being Love, Hope, Faith and Peace), was the means by which the Source of Being could be known: 'Through her (i.e. Gnosis) we know the First Father through whom we exist, the Mystery of Silence which speaks before all things, which is hidden; the First Monad through which the Pleroma became Substance.'

---

[67] See 'Extracts from the Gnostic Papyrus' (p. 44 *et. seq.*) in Soror S.S.D.D. (Florence Farr): *Collectanea Hermetica Volume VIII*, (*Egyptian Magic*) Theosophical Publishing Society, London, 1896.

In the *Bruce Codex*, Christ's function is to 're-establish the Pleroma', that is, to awaken man's knowledge of his Divine Source, ignorance of which had resulted when the Supernal Aeons were cleft from Man's grasp during the Fall. One aspect of this ignorance was man's failure to distinguish between reality and illusion, expressed in Gnostic terms as the division between true existence (Aionios) or good, and false existence (Hyle) or evil. Christ, in his own being, provided the symbol which united the two opposites, and constituted the mediating intelligence which men could aspire to in transforming themselves from mortals into Gods.

Christ's role, however, was also one of *initiator* for, according to the Codex, he related to his disciples the 'mysteries' concerning those celestial hierarchies which the soul would encounter in the after-death state:

> 'Gather round me, O my Disciples, men and women, so that I may tell you the mysteries of the Aeon of Treasure hidden in the Invisible God, which no man knoweth; and if you perform them the Aeons of the Invisible God will not be able to rise up against you, for they are great mysteries of the Holy of Holies. If you perform them the Arkhons (Rulers) of the Aeons cannot resist them nor torture you; but the Paralèmptès (Creative force) of the Aeon of Treasure can draw the soul from the body, so that it can traverse all the Aeons and the abode of the Invisible God, and lead it unto the Aeon of Treasure. And all conscious or unconscious sin shall be wiped out; a pure light shall be evolved; and the soul passing from world to world shall rest in it until it arrives at the Aeon of Treasure. Then it shall pass into the Sanctuary of the Guardians of the Aeon of Treasure; beyond this to the Sanctuary of the three Amen; beyond this to the Sanctuary of Gemini; beyond this to the Sanctuary of the Three Thunders; beyond this to the Sanctuary of the Five Trees; beyond this to the Sanctuary of the Seven Voices; beyond this into the Abode which is in the Sanctuary. This is the Abode of Akhōrētos (Established one) of the Aeon of Treasure. And all these hierarchies will give you their Seals and their Mysteries because your soul shall have received the mystery before being drawn forth from the body.'

Having conquered these intermediary Aeons, the disciples in

their new Wisdom would become 'Sons of the Pleroma', initiates into the Highest Truth. However, they would need the Sacred Word of Power in order to progress. Prior to revealing this to his disciples, Jesus first purified them with a triple baptismal invocation of Water, Fire and Holy Spirit. He then marked his disciples with a sacred seal and pronounced the following prayer:

> 'Hear me, oh my Father, Father of all Paternities, Infinite Light, for I invoke Thee in the incorruptible names of the Aeon of Light, Nereter, Zophoner, Zoilthozoybao, Xoybao, Amen, Amen, Amen. Hear me, oh my Father, may the Saboath Adamos and all the Arkhons (rulers) come forth and take away the iniquities of my disciples.'

Following this Jesus inscribed another sacred seal upon his followers to symbolize their newly-won purity. He said:

> 'Hear me now, in order that I may speak unto you of the going forth of your soul, since I have revealed these mysteries, their seals, and their numbers. When thou goest forth from thy body and perform the mysteries of all the Aeons and those which are in them, they shall fly before you until you come to the Six Great Aeons. They shall fly to the west and to the left hand. When you have come to the Six Aeons you will be stopped until you have received the mystery of the remission of sins, for this is the great mystery which is in the Aeon of the Holy of Holies, and giveth health to the soul. He who has received this mystery shall surpass all gods and all lords and all Aeons which are the Twelve Aeons of the Invisible God, because this is the Great Mystery of the Immutable One who is in the Aeon of the Holy of Holies. This is why all men who believe in the Son of Light must receive the mystery of the remission of sins.
>
> ... And when all the Aeons have fled before you the Light of the Purifying Aeon will purify the twelfth Aeon, so that all thy ways may be illuminated, and the Aeon of Light may manifest, that you may behold the heavens from afar and the Paths of Light. . . . When you have received these mysteries, and you go hither and thither, having gone forth from the body you will become a pure Light, and you will journey even unto the Aeon of Light.'

Jesus now provided them with the all-conquering Word of Power which would ensure victory over all Aeons encountered in the after-death journey,

> 'the Name of the Great Force which is in all worlds. If you speak the word, all the Worlds must submit. Those which are in the Aeons from the first to the last, even unto the Treasure of the God of Truth. The Guardians, the Hierarchies, and the Firmaments shall open before you; this is the name which I tell unto you:
> AAAŌŌŌZŌRAZAZZZAIEŌZAZAEEEIIIZAIEŌZŌAK-HŌEOOOYTHŌEZAOZAEZĒĒĒZZĒĒZAOZAKHŌZAĒK HEYEITYXAALETHYKH.
> This is the Name which you must speak in the interior world; the Name of the God of Truth is an exterior world. Live then in the exterior world, pronounce this name, mark yourself with the seal of which the Name is ZZEEŌŌKHAAAEZAZA. Say it and take in your hands the number Zonstth. When you have arrived at your destination, pronounce this name, say it first, then turn towards the four quarters of the Holy Place, make the sign of the Seal, say the name of which you hold the number in your hands.'

We also find extensive references to the esoteric role of Christ in the remarkable treatise '*Lefefa Sedek*', an Ethiopian Book of the Dead,[68] which probably dates from the fourth century A.D. and which parallels Christian Gnosticism. Christ appears to Mary in Paradise, where she is overwhelmed by the misery and torture of those who have fallen short of the Garden of Righteousness and whom she can see enslaved in the River of Fire.[69] Mary seeks and gains Christ's secret 'names of power' which will provide a protection for future deceased souls and render them immune from the hell-flames of Sheol. These revelations constitute an integral part of the sacred texts incorporated into the '*Lefefa Sedek*' and which were supposed to allow the soul safe passage to Heaven.[70]

If Zarathrustra's direct influence on the West is difficult to gauge due to Alexander's plunder of Persepolis and the Persian religion, and although Mohammed's enlightenment encompasses an inclination towards brute force, it would appear that both have nevertheless contributed to some extent. Zoroastrian ideas appear to have filtered into some of the Gnostic communities

---

[68] Translated as *The Bandlet of Righteousness* by Sir E. A. Wallis Budge. Luzac, London, 1929 (limited edition).

[69] The Gnostics (see also the *Pistis Sophia*) seem to have taken their conception of Hell from the Egyptians, Hebrews and Greeks. The result is a purgatory containing rivers of fire, serpents, and 'guardians' made up of various bestial combinations. As in the Egyptian System, which is detailed in a later section of this book, these 'guardians' change their ascendancy and form according to the twelve divisions of the outer darkness (the twelve 'hours' of the Tuat).

[70] Having gained permission from God the Father to reveal these holy names, Jesus writes them with a pen of gold: 'And a light came and hovered over them, and they (God and Christ) made seven veils of Fire round about them and none knew and none heard, neither the angels nor the archangels, until they had told Mary the whole of the following words.'

And Christ said unto her, 'Take this (Book) which I have given unto thee. And thou shalt not reveal it to the man who is not able to bear it, to keep or guard over this Book, but (only) to the wise who believe in Me and who walk in My commandments. And whosoever hath gotten possession of this Book, shall neither descend into the place of torment nor into Sheol' (Budge trans., p. 63).

There follow one hundred and ninety-two sacred names of Jesus and the seven great names of God. Finally Mary beseeches Christ to reveal his most powerful, hidden name. Standing on a pillar of cloud, enshrouded in 'a flame of fire', He proclaims:

> 'The Name of the Father is Maryal.
> The Name of the Son is Menater
> The Name of the Holy Ghost is Abayater.'
> (Budge trans., p. 74).

and enjoyed great popularity there, and during the Babylonian captivity they may have introduced into the Jewish religion the concepts of the immortality and judgement of the soul, purgatory, and the resurrection of the dead, as Maeterlinck believes.[71] Similarly Islam outlines an impressive pantheon of archangels and fire-elementals, and may have drawn on sources similar to the ancient Jewish Qabalah.

It is clear that whatever importance may be attached to one religion or religious interpretation as opposed to another, the aspect of authority or 'revelation' stems from the heightened, mystical awareness of reality achieved by its founder. Such is the role of the avatar. However, the mystical experience is not exclusive to founders of religions. It occurs in all walks of Life, to any who allow their consciousness to be exalted, to those who penetrate beyond appearances. Plato visualized a deep cave in which prisoners saw only flickering shadows of what was happening outside, and therefore confused the shadow, which was their only experience, with reality. For Plato, the shadow is a mere indicator, and extended metaphorically becomes a symbol of greater awareness.

Thomas Traherne had a similar conviction. He writes: 'The corn was orient and immortal wheat, which never should be reaped, nor was ever sown. I thought it had stood from everlasting to everlasting. The dust and the stones of the street were as precious as gold; the gates were at first the end of the world. The green trees when I saw them first through one of the gates, transported and ravished me, their sweetness and unusual beauty made my heart leap, and almost mad with ecstasy, they were such strange and wonderful things. The men! O what venerable and reverend creatures did the aged seem! Immortal Cherubim! And the young men glittering and sparkling angels and maids, strange seraphic pieces of life and beauty. Boys and girls tumbling in the street, and playing, were moving jewels ... I knew not that they were born or should die. But all things

[71] M. Maeterlinck: *The Great Secret*. University Books, New York, 1969. p. 116.

abided eternally as they were in their proper places. Eternity was manifested in the Light of Day, and something infinite behind everything appeared.'[72]

The much-quoted author of *Cosmic Consciousness*, Dr. R. M. Bucke, describes an experience he had while driving home after a pleasant discussion with friends about poetry and philosophy:

'His mind, deeply under the influence of the ideas, images and emotions called up by the reading and talk of the evening, was calm and peaceful. He was in a state of quiet, almost passive enjoyment. All at once, without warning of any kind, he found himself wrapped around as it were by a flame-coloured cloud. For an instant he thought of fire, some sudden conflagration in the great city; the next he knew that the light was within himself. Directly afterwards there came upon him a sense of exultation, of immense joyousness accompanied or immediately followed by an intellectual illumination quite impossible to describe. Into his brain streamed one momentary lightning-flash of the Brahmic Splendour which has ever since lightened his life. . . . Among other things, he did not come to believe, he saw and knew that the cosmos is not dead matter but a living Presence. . . .'[73]

George Russell, the great Irish mystic who wrote under the initials A.E., had a similar experience of the Infinite Logos, although his was more personified. He felt surrounded by spiritual presences.

'As I walked in the evening down the lane scented by the honeysuckle my senses were expectant of some unveiling about to take place. I felt that beings were looking in upon me out of the true home of man. They seemed to be saying to each of us "Soon they will awaken; soon they will come to us again", and for a moment I almost seemed to mix with their eternity. The tinted air glowed before me with intelligible significance like a

---

[72] Thomas Traherne: *Works*.
[73] Written by Bucke in the third person. See also Kenneth Walker: *Diagnosis of Man*, Pelican Books, Harmondsworth, 1962, pp. 163 *et. seq.*

face, a voice. The visible world became like a tapestry blown and stirred by wind behind it. If it would but raise for an instant I knew I would be in Paradise. Every form on that tapestry appeared to be the work of gods.'[74] For Russell the experience arouses a pantheistic awareness where Nature is saturated with meaning. He felt swept up into Infinity, and in union with greater beings.

This feeling of unity and harmony is one of the hallmarks of mystical consciousness, the type of awareness of oneness with Nature which Edward Carpenter called 'Universal Consciousness'. In his book *The Act of Creation* he wrote: 'This form of consciousness is the only true knowledge—it is the only true existence.'[75] It was for him a type of perception where the observer and observed blend into one. At such a level a man does not so much think as *become* those things which he perceives and without motion, without change, without effort, without distinction of subject and object but with vast and incredible joy.

[74] A. E. (George Russell): *The Candle of Vision*. Macmillan, London, 1920, pp. 5–6.
[75] Edward Carpenter: *The Act of Creation*. Allen & Unwin, London, 1907.

CHAPTER THREE

The Symbolism of Magic

Up till now we have dealt with related mystical and religious concepts rather than with magic itself. As a subject, the latter has been accorded insufficient respect by those people who insist unjustifiably on coupling it with various brands of witchcraft and medieval superstition: magic in its purest form has nothing in common with these. It is more correctly compared with the highest types of mystical religion, for it derives its practices and tradition from the esoteric teachings of all that was sacred in ancient Egypt and the Near East, and in particular from those mystical emanationist systems which form the basis of Gnosticism and the Qabalah.

In one important way, however, High Magic may be distinguished from those types of pantheistic mysticism mentioned earlier. It is clearly not a passive system, but an active one. The onus is placed squarely upon the magician to develop, through his own Will, the means of communication with his Higher Self, and identification with different aspects of the Godhead. It is a system whereby the consciousness is enlarged stage by stage, as the individual increasingly gains control of the neglected realms of the unconscious psyche.

The basic premise behind such an approach is that man in essence contains the whole Universe, in the same way that a drop of water resembles the Ocean. Self-knowledge allows the individual to burst his confines and to become truly cosmic. This experience of Unity with the One exactly parallels that described by A.E., Thomas Traherne and Dr. R. M. Bucke. But it is a

THE SYMBOLISM OF MAGIC

Union *directed by the Will* rather than a passive state of mind occurring randomly and without intent.

Israel Regardie, the modern occultist and one-time pupil of Aleister Crowley, is widely considered to be one of the greatest living authorities on High Magic and the function of ritual. A member of the Stella Matutina (a derivative of the Hermetic Order of the Golden Dawn) he has published the definitive collection of its ritual practices. In his classic work *The Tree of Life* he writes: 'The Magician must be in control of the whole of his nature; every constituent element in his being must be developed under Will to the topmost pitch of perfection.'[76]

This statement necessitates the question: what then is man's nature?

Traditionally ritual magic has drawn upon the Qabalah, the most comprehensive system of Western mysticism, for its answers.

The Qabalah has been fully discussed in many fine specialist volumes and cannot be justly summarised in a few paragraphs. However, the system as such involves a multiple symbol, Otz Chiim[76A] or the Tree of Life which consists of ten spheres of Being through which Creation proceeds. These spheres or Sephiroth align themselves in three columns headed by the Supernals, Kether, Chokmah and Binah, and constitute a symbolic portrayal of the vibrant emanations of the Godhead, the Unmanifest becoming manifest. Man in the Qabalistic view is thus more than he seems, for, like the whole of Nature, he is an end result of a Cosmic process which unfolds by stages and degrees. He is made up of not only his physical body but a spiritual counterpart which gave rise to it, a design which has gradually fulfilled itself as a form.

---

[76] Israel Regardie: *The Tree of Life*. Rider, London, 1932, p. 36.
[76A] The Hebrew for the Tree of Life is *Ayin, Tsaddi, Cheth, Yod, Yod, Mem* (עץ חיים). This has by many commentators been transliterated as *Otz Chiim*, which has the advantage of identifying the component Hebrew letters (especially when printed OTz ChIIM) but the disadvantage of giving a totally incorrect idea of the pronunciation, which depends on the pointing of the letters. The pronounciation is better represented by *Ets Ḥayyim*.

The Qabalists align the ten Sephiroth into four major planes of creative manifestation. The highest of these is the spiritual level called Atziluth, the world of archetypes, the very essence of all creation. Beneath this plane, in Briah, these archetypes begin to crystallise into specific ideas, and in Yetzirah definite forms appear whose familiar counterparts may be found in the archetypal images of the unconscious mind. In the fourth world, Assiah, the manifesting forms of creation finally become real in the sense we know them normally. Man as a created being necessarily has a spiritual counterpart at all of these levels. However, his limited awareness prevents him from experiencing the different planes of consciousness at will and from integrating such knowledge into his concept of himself. It is this self-knowledge which the magician pursues, for it is in this manner that man re-acquires his lost divinity and becomes a God.[77] The spiritual awakening involves knowledge of man's inner self, in fact, a knowledge of the nature of his 'soul' if we may be permitted to use that much maligned term. In the Qabalistic system the 'soul' may be divided into three parts: Neschamah, Ruach and Nephesch. These equate with certain vehicles of higher consciousness, and as such correlate with different Sephirothic emanations. Thus Neschamah is the highest point of being, deriving from the Supernals, Kether Chokmah and Binah.[78] Lying above the Abyss, its source is in the domain of the pure Godhead and lies for all practical purposes outside the scope of ritual magic.[79] Beneath this level is the Ruach aspect of the soul which equates with the Higher Astral planes of the unconscious mind and incorporate that range of existence between the Sephiroth Chesed and Hod. 'The unconscious with its fertility of impressive ideas and suggestions may be for

---

[77] In the words of Christ: 'The Kingdom of God is within you. . . . Ye shall be as gods.'

[78] More accurately, Neschamah relates to the specific Sephirah Binah. Two other aspects, Yechidah and Chiah, derive from Kether and Chokmah respectively.

[79] For this reason we would disagree with Regardie's correlation (in the *Middle Pillar*) of the Supernals with the Jungian Unconscious. Most of the solar-myth archetypes are clearly derived from Tiphareth, one of the Ruach Sephiroth.

some people the source of poetic and artistic inspiration', writes Regardie, and we have endeavoured to point out certain Sephirothic origins in our earlier work on those Surrealist artists who attempted to merge the dream and its unconscious contents with the three-dimensionality of the normal experience, (painters like Max Ernst, Yves Tanguy and Réné Magritte).[80] Some artists of this school, however, allowed the more animalian aspects of the Unconscious to predominate, and it is this instinctual characteristic of the soul which is termed Nephesch and which correlates with the Ninth Sephirah, Yesod.[81] Austin Spare, the extraordinary artist-occultist, was particularly prone to the inspiration of the Nephesch and allowed animal forms which he regarded as his earlier incarnations, to possess his consciousness. Salvador Dali and Felix Labisse, among others, are examples of Surrealists who have similarly drawn on Nephesch inspiration particularly in its relationship to Yesod, which is the Chakra corresponding with the genitals and the centre of the Freudian sex-instinct. The tenth Sephirah, Malkuth is the seat of the physical organism, with the brain as vehicle of consciousness.

It is clear that if the magician is to 'know himself' he must retrace his identity to its highest sources and thus transform both his range of perception, and ultimately himself, in so doing.

We have indicated that one factor common to all magical and religious systems is the belief in supernatural beings. For the magician these beings do not only exist, *they are encountered*. They are symptomatic of man's intrinsic capacity to personify what would otherwise be quite inconceivable, and, as archetypes they are experienced at all levels of higher consciousness. For example, in the immediate spheres of the unconscious, in Malkuth, the magician encounters the personifications of the four Elements: the gnomes of the Earth; the Sylphs of the Air;

---

[80] See '*The Search for Abraxas*', Neville Spearman, London, 1973.
[81] In *the Golden Dawn*, Regardie identifies it with Malkuth, but in *The Middle Pillar*, with Yesod. The latter would seem to be more appropriate.

the Undines of Water, and the Salamanders of Fire. There are, in fact, four symbolic divisions within each Sephirah and these align with the four 'worlds' or planes of Atziluth, Briah, Yetzirah and Assiah, already mentioned. That is to say that within Malkuth, for example, the level of Assiah (the so-called 'Mundane Chakra') manifests as a personification of the Elements (Gnomes, etc.). At a higher level within this Sephirah there occur visions of the ascribed God, Adonai ha Aretz in Atziluth, the Archangel Sandalphon in Briah, and the Angelic Choirs, Ashim, or Souls of Fire, in Yetzirah. These visions are marked by specific colour combinations which in the four worlds within Malkuth are as follows:

Atziluth: Yellow.
Briah: Citrine, olive, russet and black.
Yetzirah: Citrine, olive, russet and black, flecked with gold.
Assiah: Black rayed with yellow.[82]

When Israel Regardie makes the claim that 'the object of Magic ... is the return of man to the Gods'[83] he is not postulating a revival of pagan worship but refers only to the way in which the theurgist rediscovers his inner realms of being, and identifies with their symbols. The basis of Magic is the fulfilment of human consciousness but it must be remembered that there is only ONE SPIRIT, ONE INTELLIGENCE which pervades the whole Universe. Man must therefore identify with his Source.

'From the unknown, incomprehensible Darkness (i.e. non-manifestation) which is Ain Soph there is but one indivisible consciousness alike in the lowliest dog-faced demon as in the greatest celestial hierarchy. There are hierarchies of consciousness which are celestial and there are those which are terrestrial; some divine, other demoniac, and still others including the highest Gods and Universal Essences.'[84] It is in such a way that polytheism and monotheism fuse, for 'the whole Universe is

---

[82] A table of the Sephiroth and their attributions is provided in Appendix B.
[83] Israel Regardie: *The Tree of Life*, p. 58.
[84] Israel Regardie: *The Tree of Life*, p. 57.

permeated by One Life, and that Life in manifestation is represented by hosts of mighty Gods, divine beings, cosmic spirits or intelligences. . . .'[85]

It is probable that the distinction between monotheism and polytheism has been overplayed by those who would wish to brand certain earlier religions as inferior and pagan. In Wallis Budge's view, the religion of ancient Egypt was essentially monotheistic despite its elaborate pantheon of deities. He writes: 'All the gods of all the great companies of Gods were only the names of the attributes and powers of the great Sun-god, whether he was called Khepera, Neb-Er-Djer, Tem, Ra, or Amen.'[86] And in Chapter XVII of *The Egyptian Book of the Dead* Osiris tells the scribe Ani: 'I am the great god who created himself . . . who made his names to become the company of the gods as god . . . I am he who is not driven back among the gods. . . .'[87]

Greek and Roman pantheons similarly personify their focal point in the Father deities Zeus and Jupiter.

According to one's view the Gods may be seen as external to man or simply as an extension of his own psychic universe. In this connection, one aspect which needs to be stressed is that Tiphareth, the sixth Sephirah, symbolizes the rebirth of man (the essence of initiation) and at the Abyss the individual ego 'dies' completely and the real, Higher Self emerges in rapport with its Cosmic Source. The realisation of Unity with *all* the manifestations and emanations of the Godhead becomes apparent because the Self is no longer outside them. It is only the ego which insists that we are unique. So if we assign Gods to a specific plane where they appear to act as objective realities, it is primarily the result of an inbuilt tendency whereby the human mind forms anthropomorphic conceptions of celestial intelligences greater than itself. Jung has alluded to

[85] Israel Regardie: *The Tree of Life*, p. 57.
[86] E. A. Wallis Budge: *The Bandlet of Righteousness*, pp. 6–7.
[87] E. A. Wallis Budge: *The Egyptian Book of the Dead*, Routledge & Kegan Paul, London. Second edition (Eighth impression) 1960.

'the relative autonomy of the archetypes',[88] but the fact that the Gods impress the visionary with their superlative qualities should not belie the fact that at a higher level they all proceed as emanations from one source of *being*.

The Magus thus becomes the vehicle for the manifesting god; he allows the sublime energies of Atziluth to envelope his own Assiatic framework; he experiences the 'union between (his own) lesser consciousness . . . and the greater consciousness of the God'. It is evident that as the individual becomes aware of the more sublime Sephirothic levels he rejects his lower self in favour of his higher being. In this way the so-called 'false ego' is 'offered up in sacrifice to the Holy Guardian Angel' (the Higher Self).[89] It is the spiritual conversation with, and knowledge of, this Holy Guardian Angel which constitutes the main task of the Magician.

This uplifting is naturally a difficult process since it runs counter to the aspirations of the ego, which attempts to maintain dominance of the Self. For this reason, Magicians have developed aids for the elevation of consciousness. These aids include symbolic gestures and expressions which, together with certain implements, form the Magical ritual. The ritual itself includes 'a deliberate exhilaration of the Will and the exhaltation of the Imagination, the end being the purification of the personality and the attainment of a spiritual state of consciousness'.[90]

Now, because the consciousness of the Magician is to be transformed in its entirety, the ritual must enhance all the senses in fine degree. The way in which this is done can be summarised as follows:

SIGHT: The ritual robes, actions and implements are a visual representation relevant to the specific end which is sought. In this drama colours and symbols play a paramount role.
SOUND: This involves the vibration of good names, chants or

---

[88] C. G. Jung (ed): *Man and his Symbols*, p. 65.
[89] Israel Regardie: *The Tree of Life*, p. 78.
[90] Israel Regardie: *The Tree of Life*, p. 106.

mantras whose auditory rhythms have a profound effect on the consciousness.

TASTE: This may take the form of a sacrament which relates symbolically to the nature of the god-form in the ritual.

SMELL: Incense and perfumes may be used both to channel the atmosphere into rapport with a specific deity or being, and also, in certain circumstances, to provide the basis (fine particles of suspended liquid) for a manifestation.

TOUCH: This is developed at a level outside the physical organism since assimilation with god-forms takes place in the Body of Light. This simulacrum performs functions parallel to those undertaken on the physical plane, although the range of perception is of a different order.

Before discussing in detail the specific ritual objects, a related point needs to be stressed and that is that *sound* and the *power of the utterance* have been traditionally emphasised as being most important.

This applies to both magic and religion. In the opening paragraph of the Book of John (I, i) it is written: 'In the beginning was the Word, and the Word was with God, and the Word was God. He was in the beginning with God; all things were made through Him, and without Him was not anything made that was made.' Again in Psalms (XXIX, iii) we find the reference: 'The voice of the Lord is upon the waters'.

According to the Qabalistic *Zohar*, or *Book of Splendour*, the world was formed by the utterance of the Sacred Name of God, a forty-two letter extension of the Tetragrammaton YHVH (Yod, He, Vau, He). The Word or Logos thus permeates the whole mystical act of Creation.[91] The ritual Magician takes a similar view. Franz Bardon says: 'The divine names are symbolic designations of divine qualities and powers',[92] and Eliphas Levi writes in his *The Key of the Mysteries* that 'all Magic is in a word, and that word pronounced Qabalistically

---

[91] We are reminded that the Zohar constitutes, as one of its functions, an esoteric commentary on Genesis.

[92] Franz Bardon: *The Practice of Magical Evocation*. Rudolf Pravica, Graz-Puntigam Austria, 1967, p. 20.

is stronger than all the powers of Heaven, Earth and Hell'.[93]

There is a reason for this emphasis on sound and on the uttered name for in many ancient traditions the name was regarded as the *very essence of being*. The early Ethiopians, whose sacred book *Lefefa Sedek* has already been mentioned, argued that God had created Himself and the Universe through the utterance of His own name and therefore 'the Name of God was the Essence of God (and) . . . was not only the source of His power but also the seat of His very Life, and was to all intents and purposes His Soul'.[94] Thus we find the Virgin Mary beseeching Jesus for his secret names so that, as a source of power, they would constitute a protection for the deceased against all manner of harmful devils. Similarly in the *Egyptian Book of the Dead* the newcomer to the Hall of Maati says to Osiris: 'I know thee. I know thy name. I know the names of the two-and-forty gods who are with thee.'[95] For it follows that he who knows the secret name, strikes home at the heart of the matter; he is in control, the essence of the god is in his very grasp. Budge writes: 'The Knowledge of the name of a god enabled a man not only to free himself from the power of that god, but to use that name as a means of obtaining what he himself wanted without considering the god's will.'[96]

The Gnostics, who borrowed heavily from Egyptian sources, believed that a knowledge of the names of the intermediary dieties and devils was essential if the soul were to return to its divine origin in the Great Aeon. An obvious characteristic of such esoteric tracts as the Tibetan, Egyptian and Ethiopian Books of the Dead and the *Pistis Sophia*, is that the contents relate profoundly to the after-death state. However, as has been mentioned elsewhere, the whole concept of the Body of Light, Initiation, and the Second Birth, refers to a state of

---

[93] Rider and Company, London, 1959 (trans. A. Crowley).
[94] E. A. Wallis Budge: *The Bandlet of Righteousness*, p. 3.
[95] E. A. Wallis Budge: Ibid. p. 4.
[96] E. A. Wallis Budge: Ibid., p. 5.

out-of-the-body consciousness which parallels the after-death experience. Furthermore it is undoubtedly true that the name, *per se*, is one of the intrinsic qualities of the encountered deities. The extract from the *Pistis Sophia* quoted earlier, which names the rulers of the Twelve dungeons of the Outer Darkness, provides us with a clue. Archaroch and Achrocar are Temura-equivalents[97] with Charachar and Archeoch as close parallels, and a similar relationship exists between Luchar and Laroch. Clearly, the rhythmic vibratory patterns of the appellations themselves are related to the very nature of these devils on the astral plane, for the utterance of such symbolic names is sufficient to dispel them.

Returning to the nature of ritual we can say that it invariably involves the invocation of beings or forces through the spoken word. However, it also relates strongly to Will, which we have already hallmarked as a factor distinguishing magic from passive forms of mysticism.

In ritual groups it is normal for members to take a magical name. Aleister Crowley's was 'Perdurabo' (I will endure to the end), and Macgregor Mathers' motto was 'S. Rhiogail Mo Dhream' (Royal is my tribe).[98] And as Crowley himself says: 'Words should express will: hence the Mystic Name of the Probationer is the expression of his highest Will.'[99] That is to say it epitomises the will of the Magician to communicate with the Higher Self or Holy Guardian Angel. Dion Fortune, who was a member of the Golden Dawn, found the projection of her Body of Light much easier when she was given her magical name. Presumably it enabled her to focus her Will more effectively. She writes: 'In my own experience of the operation, the utterance to myself of my Magical name led to the picturing of myself in an idealised form, not differing in type, but upon an altogether grander

---

[97] Temura is a method of changing the position of letters in a word, to create a new word which relates in meaning to the original.
[98] Another of Mathers' dicta was: 'There is no part of me which is not of the Gods' which resembles a line from the Egyptian *Papyrus of Nu*: 'There is no member of my body which is not a member of a god'.
[99] Aleister Crowley: *Book Four*, Pt. II, p. 42.

scale, superhuman in fact, but recognisable as myself, as a statue more than life-size may yet be a good likeness. Once perceived, I could re-picture this idealised version of my body and personality at will, but I could not identify myself with it *unless I uttered my Magical name.* Upon my affirming it as my own, identification was immediate.'[100]

Thus the higher vision of the Self supercedes the more limited scope of the ego and the process of spiritual transformation begins. 'Ultimately,' writes Crowley, 'the Magical Will so identifies itself with the (individual's) whole being that it becomes unconscious,'[101] That is to say the Union is no longer an aim, but a reality.

We turn now to the actual symbols of ritual Magic whereby this transformation is achieved. The first of these is the place of the Working itself, the Temple.

The Temple contains all magical actions; it therefore represents the entire Universe and, by inference, the Magician himself, because of the relationship of macrocosm to microcosm. Upon the floor of the Temple are certain inscriptions; the most important of which is the circle. *The Circle* incorporates many symbolic meanings but most importantly it represents the Infinite Godhead, the Alpha and Omega, the Divine Self-Knowledge which the magician aspires to. As a symbol of *what he may become* the Circle indicates *invocation* rather than *evocation*. By standing in the centre of the Circle, the magician is able to identify with the source of Creation, and consequently his Will ensures that the ego-devils of his lesser self remain outside the 'sphere' of higher consciousness. The magician now takes on a role of authority in the sense that he intends to subject the invoked deity to his Will. The God-names, which have already been mentioned, are of vital importance in this respect. Inscribed around the periphery of the Circle, these holy names stipulate the exact nature of the working. In addition, the Circle may be circumscribed by an equal-sided geometrical

[100] Dion Fortune: *Applied Magic* Aquarian Press, London, 1962, pp. 56–7.
[101] Aleister Crowley: *Book Four*, Pt. II, p. 46.

figure whose number of sides correspond with the Sephirah appropriate to the God (e.g. a hexagram in the case of Tiphareth (Osiris). The circle also contains a Tau which, as an assertive, masculine symbol balances the receptive or passive role of the Circle itself, the two together constitute a balance of opposites, the Spiritual Marriage or Great Work. The Tau is made up of ten squares, one for each Sephirah, and is usually vermillion in colour, as are the inscribed God names; the Circle area is complementary green. Nine equidistant pentagrams, each containing a small glowing lamp, surround the Circle, the tenth and most important Lamp hanging above the centre. (This will be mentioned separately).

The Circle must, of course, be large enough for the magus to move around in for he must not leave it during invocation. Otherwise its powers as a focus of the Will are destroyed.

In terms of construction, where the Circle is not a permanent fixture of the Temple floor, it may be chalked in colour, or sewn or printed on cloth. Whenever the Circle is already in existence its sacred nature must be reaffirmed in the mind of the magician, for otherwise the Circle remains a purely profane symbol. The magician thus traces over its inscribed form with his ritual sword or outstretched hand at the same time considering carefully the symbolic meaning of his action. In the final instance, if conditions for a Temple working do not exist, the Circle may be inscribed upon the ground (in the case of outdoor workings) or held within the imagination, as in the case of the Banishing Ritual of the lesser Pentagram. The strength of this latter type of Circle naturally depends upon the magician's powers of visualization.

The Triangle needs to be mentioned now, primarily because of its essentially opposite role. Unlike the Circle, which connotes the Infinite, the Triangle stands for finite manifestation, that which already exists. Symbolic of the triadic nature of creation and the union of astral, mental and physical levels, the Triangle represents *evocation*. Like the Circle, it must be carefully constructed or mentally re-inforced to impress the mind of the Magus. In like fashion, the Triangle must restrain the evoked being, for otherwise the Magician may lose control of the manifestation and may even find himself mentally conquered by it, that is to say, obsessed. The talisman placed in the centre of the Triangle incorporates the seal, or sign of the spirit and provides the focus of the ritual.[102]

Returning to the nature of *in*vocation, which is of primary concern to us here, certain magical implements may be employed by the magician within the Magic Circle. Most of these reside upon the central *Altar*, which symbolises the foundation of the ritual the Magical Will itself.

Consisting of a double cube of wood[103], the Altar has ten exposed faces, corresponding with the ten Sephiroth upon the Tree of Life. The lowest face is Malkuth, the Kingdom, which represents things as they are. The upper face is Kether, the Crown, the First-Manifest, and Crowley recommends that it be plated with gold, the metal of perfection. Upon the sides of the Altar, he adds, should be written 'the sigils of the holy Elemental Kings'.[104]

Placed upon the Altar are certain symbolic implements designed to channel the imagination into a state of transcendence. These may be summarised as follows:

The Holy Oil: This golden fluid is ideally contained in a vessel of rock-crystal, and in using it, the magician anoints the Four points of the Microcosm (Kether, Gedulah, Geburah and Malkuth) upon his forehead, left and right shoulders and solar plexus respectively, at the same time reminding himself of the sacred nature of the task ahead. The holy ointment itself consists of the oils of the olive, myrrh, cinnamon and galangual, these representing in turn Chokmah (the Logos; Wisdom); Binah (Understanding); Tiphareth (Harmony, Spiritual Awakening) and Kether-Malkuth (the Greater

---

[102] Descriptive details of spirits and elementals may be found in Franz Bardon's *The Practice of Magical Evocation*.
[103] Usually acacia or oak.
[104] Aleister Crowley: *Book Four*, Pt. II, p. 23.

THE SYMBOLISM OF MAGIC

and Lesser Countenance, the Union of Being and Created).

The Wand: This, like the Altar, symbolises the pursuit of Higher Wisdom (Chokmah) achieved through the Will. Its tip is Kether, the ambivalent first Sephirah which contains the Union of opposites, the conquest of duality in all its forms.[105] In the Golden Dawn a *Lotus Wand* was used which was multi-coloured, with its upper end white and its lower, black. In between were twelve bands of colour corresponding to the astrological divisions:

White

Red	Aries
Red-orange	Taurus
Orange	Gemini
Amber	Cancer
Lemon Yellow	Leo
Yellow-Green	Virgo
Emerald	Libra
Green-Blue	Scorpio
Blue	Sagittarius
Indigo	Capricorn
Violet	Aquarius
Purple	Pisces

Black

The lotus flower, with three whorls of petals was placed upon the tip of the wand, the white end being used for invocation, the black end for banishing.

Franz Bardon suggests a similar procedure except that he substitutes, instead, bands of metal whose Sephirothic attributes align with the seven planets:

(White) *Silver*	Moon	Yesod
Brass	Mercury	Hod

[105] Kether is the highest point on the Middle Pillar and incorporates, as Monad, all other emanations, and both polarities.

APPROACHES

	Copper	Venus	Netzach
	Gold	Sun	Tiphareth
	Iron/Steel	Mars	Geburah
	Tin	Jupiter	Gedulah/Chesed
(Black)	Lead	Saturn	Binah

The *Wand* may be made of wood (especially ash, oak or acacia) or magnetised electro-steel (nickel-plated for protection). In the latter case, the North and South poles should be identified and marked positive and negative. The magician may have different wands for varying magical purposes, and like all other magical implements, they should be insulated in silk cloth when not in use.

The Wand represents the first letter, Yod, of the Tetragrammator YHVH, and also the Element Fire. The ritual objects immediately following, the Cup, Sword and Pentacle, complete this Sacred Name of God and represent the Elements Water, Air and Earth respectively.

The Cup: As a feminine, receptive symbol, the Cup aligns with Binah, the Mother of Understanding. The Magician must gradually fill his cup of consciousness with an understanding and knowledge of his Higher Self. As a symbol of containment rather than of Becoming, the Cup is not of practical importance in invocation, but may be used in rituals of manifestation.

The Sword: Indicative of the Magician's vital victory, or mastery over the invoked or evoked powers, the Sword (human force) equates to some extent with the Wand (Divine power). Suggestive of control and therefore order, it implies Reason, the offspring of Wisdom and Understanding. It is therefore attributed to Tiphareth[106], the sphere of Harmony. The symmetry of the Sword is correspondingly appropriate. According to Aleister Crowley, the guard should consist of two moons waxing and waning, affixed back to back (Yesod); the blade should be made of steel (corresponding to Mars), and the

---

[106] Tiphareth is the focus of the Ruach.

hilt should be constructed of copper (symbolic of Venus) indicating that ultimately the Sword is subject to the all-encompassing principle of Love. When the Sword is placed representationally upon the Tree of Life, the pommel rests in Daath,[107] gateway to the Supernals; the points of the guard is Chesed (Gedulah) and Geburah; and the tip in Malkuth. Crowley makes the important observation that 'the Magician cannot wield the Sword unless the Crown is on his head'; force and aspiration without *inspiration* are of no avail.

The Pentacle: In the same way that the Sword corresponds to the Wand, so the Pentacle is the 'other half' of the Cup. Symbolic of Malkuth, the Heavenly Daughter and goddess of the manifest universe, the Pentacle or Disc, is designed to 'induce awe' in the magician. Malkuth, the culmination of the process of Creation instigated in Kether, constitutes the first step of the Mystical Journey back to the Supernals. The Pentacle is thus the Body of the Magician, which he would wish to be filled with the Holy Ghost, and it also stands for his Karma, or actual nature prior to spiritual transformation.

We turn now to the Magician himself who wears upon his head *The Crown*, or headband, representative of Kether and the Fulfilment of the Great Work. Made of gold it is a symbol of aspiration to the Divine.

Over his body falls *The Robe* whose function is to protect the Magus from adverse 'astral' influences. For this reason the robed (and hooded) figure is recommended as the mental form of the Body of Light. Normally black in colour The Robe symbolises anonymity and silence and is the dark vessel into which Light is poured. Attached or sewn to it across the chest is *The Lamen*, the 'breastplate' which protects the heart (Tiphareth). In the same way that Tiphareth is the focal point of all the Sephiroth, the Lamen should have inscribed upon it symbols which relate to all aspects of the Magical Purpose. An active form of the passive Pentacle, the Lamen indicates

---

[107] Daath is not represented by a Sephirah but constitutes the Abyss between the Supernal Triad and the lower emanations of the Tree of Life.

strength. So too does the *Magical Book* which the Magician holds in his hands. This contains the entire Magical details of ritual aims and practice; it is in a sense, a history of the unfolding of the effects of his Magical Will. As such it constitutes a steadfast symbol of power and determination.

In addition, the Magician may employ the use of a *Bell* worn on a chain around the neck. 'This Bell summons and alarms', writes Regardie, 'and it is also the Bell which sounds at the elevation of the Host.' Representative of alertness, it thus alludes to the sublime 'musical note' of the Higher Spheres, which sounds in the heart of the perfected man. In this respect the symbolism of the Bell parallels that of the *Sacred Lamp* which as 'the light of the "pure soul" ' and which resides *above* the ritual implements and represents the descent of Spirit into Form, Light into Darkness, God into Man. It stands for all that is eternal and unchanging, the first swirlings of the Primal Energy ('Let there be Light'). It is 'the Lost Word, the dying music whose sevenfold echo is IAO and AUM. Without this Light, says Crowley, the Magician could not work at all; yet few indeed are the Magicians that have known of it, and far fewer they that have beheld its brilliance.'

The Magus thus takes upon himself the enflaming of his imagination through the imagery of sacred, symbolic objects. Facing towards the East, he engages upon his encounter with the Gods. In the Eastern quarter stands the *Censer* containing red-hot coals and fuming incense; the brazier which transforms finite substance into pure, infinite energy, symbolising the manner in which the imperfect, lower, ego is to be sacrificed to the true, Higher Self.

THE PATH OF THE CHAMELEON

It is said that in the land beyond sleep there grows a Cosmic Tree which extends from the ground to the highest point of Heaven.

The warder of the Tree is a sacred dragon whose body radiates coloured lights of dazzling brilliance which change their hue as he moves from one branch to another.

Men know that Gods live under his auspices too, and that if they would wish to converse with them, they must make the mystical journey, upon *the Path of the Chameleon*.

CHAPTER ONE

The Egyptian Books of the Dead

> 'The Earth is for thy dead Body,
> and the Sky is for thy Soul . . .'
> Egyptian *Book of Gates*

The task of the Magus is, as we have seen, a regenerative one, for he must enlarge his consciousness to the point whereby his own notion of 'self' falls away, and he is reawakened, or spiritually reborn.

One of the fundamental practices of high magic is the separation of consciousness from the physical body, and its controlled projection into specific realms of the normally unconscious mind, where it encounters archetypal visions and assimilates them through a process of identification. The structure of the mind is such, that in the same way dreams tend to reflect social and cultural influences, so too the archetypes take on a form moulded by the environment. One need only look at medieval renditions of Christ to see that peoples conceive of the same archetype in different forms, although the core meaning remains the same. For this reason we differ from writers like Claude Levi Strauss who assert that deities are like words, taking their meaning solely from their context. Only the outer form is so derived; the intrinsic meaning, the mythological '*status*' of the deity, remains intact.

Because this is so, we find that many ancient pantheons, particularly the elaborate ones which cover a wide range of human perception and classification, offer a possibility of structuring the unconscious in their capacity as self-contained systems of archetypes. A god offers an example of what a man may *become*. The Australian aboriginals traditionally imitated the creation drama of the Dream-time, so that all subsequent social behaviour had, ideally, a ritual basis. In Burma, the King, and his delegated officers ruled over a Kingdom divided and structured as a reflection of the macrocosm. A given pantheon of gods may be considered, therefore, to provide a direct gauge of the highest realms of imaginative and perceptive thought capable in the society concerned, provided of course that magic or religion constitutes a dominant part of the world-view.

Not all deities have the regenerative function sought after by theurgists. In addition, few ancient (or contemporary) pantheons have direct relevance to the theurgist, for he must be able not only to reconstruct their scale of meanings and symbols but to be able to *identify* with them and to *live* them.

Western magic owes its forms primarily to four Western pantheons, the Qabalah (in which the emanations are of God, rather than gods), the Egyptian, the Graeco-Roman and the Neoplatonic—'Chaldean'. All are highly developed systems, and elaborate upon the nature of those deities which epitomise the loftiest creative abilities inherent in man, the microcosm. As symbols of the source of inspiration they are invaluable, and it is this visionary function which the magician seeks to awaken and experience.

We have indicated earlier that mystical experience and the most intense forms of insight derive from profound levels of the unconscious mind. Pantheons such as the above therefore provide us with a structure whereby the unconscious may be systematically explored. In *The Search For Abraxas* we used the term Uranography, borrowed from Thomas Fuller, to describe such a framework[108], and suggested that its practice could 'consist of systematic reawakening those extensions of conscious-

[108] Nevill Drury and Stephen Skinner. *The Search for Abraxas*. Neville Spearman. London, 1973, p. 124.

ness that for most of us appear to have been closed for ever by our civilisation or upbringing".

In the Qabalistic Tree of Life, seen as a multiple glyph representing different stages of consciousness, we find an admirably practical basis for such work. The same can be said of the ancient Egyptian funerary tests, where the journey of the deceased into the underworld, the subsequent judgement and spiritual rebirth, parallel exactly the ecsomatic journey undertaken in trance by exponents of high magic in the West.

The Greeks and Romans also had a shamanistic, or 'ecstatic' tradition which extended itself as a systematic teaching in the mystery schools of Orpheus, Dionysus, and Pythagoras, and at legendary Eleusis, sacred to Demeter and Persephone. We find references to the 'flight of the soul' in the Classical mythology and in specific accounts of legendary shamans like Aristeas of Proconnesus. And in the works of the Pythagoreans and Neoplatonists there are clear references to ecsomatic projection as a basis for initiation. The 'soul-body' assimilates certain archetypal experiences and is 'reborn' or revitalized.

In summary, we have two major forms available to us: after-death, or eschatological beliefs, presented as mythology or as teachings about the post-mortem state, and structures of emanations, which provide a framework for the mystical ascent of consciousness.

Taking the eschatological expressions first, we note that the ancient Egyptian post-mortem belief is, by common consent, both the most lucid and complete 'after-death' uranography available in the West. It represents a cumulative knowledge comparable in scope with the Tibetan *Bardo Thodol* which has been analysed by Drs Leary, Metzner and Alpert for precisely the same purpose as our own: namely to provide a structure for the spiritual rebirth of the individual[109].

We are fortunate that the ancient Egyptians chose to repre-

---

[109] Drs. Timothy Leary, Ralph Metzner and Richard Alpert. *The Psychedelic Experience*. A manual based on *The Tibetan Book of the Dead*. University Books, New York, 1964.

sent their beliefs, graphically upon the walls of tombs, and inscribed upon sarcophagi. And as Rundle Clark says: 'Egyptian gods are nearer the stark archetypes of the unconscious mind than the Greek ones, and, in a sense, they are more intellectual, too, for they are expressing ideas.'[110] Wallis Budge explains, too, that the Egyptian archetypal imagery remained relatively constant in its portrayal, for like the oral Qabalistic tradition, it was handed down as a system whose components had exact meanings:

'In cases where archetypes were available the artist was careful to follow in all general matters the ancient copies to which he had access.'[111]

Brandon cites the Egyptians as being the first to conceive of a post-mortem judgement, and since the judgement was linked with the possibility of spiritual revitalization through the beneficence of Ra, their cosmological mythology and its visual representations are of direct relevance to the western theurgist.[112]

For our purposes the two Egyptian treatises most relevant to the concept of uranography are the Osirian *Book of Gates* and the *Am-Tuat* compiled by the followers of Amen-Ra. The major difference between them is that the former stresses resurrection,[113] whereby the spiritual company of Osiris spend

---

[110] R. T. Rundle Clark: *Myth and Symbol in Ancient Egypt*. Thames & Hudson, London, 1959, p. 12.

[111] Wallis Budge: *The Egyptian Heaven and Hell*. Martin Hopkinson, London, 1925, (Commentary) p. 2.

[112] Text in fact preceded illustration in the description of Egyptian eschatology. The earliest religions compositions are found in the pyramids of Unas, Teta, Pepi I, Mer-en-Ra, and Pepi II, and have no illustrations despite the fact that some earlier mastabas (tombs) had coloured bas-relief.

[113] The Egyptian conception of resurrection is well expressed in the famous myth of Osiris, his wife and sister Isis and his jealous brother Set.

Set was said to have invited Osiris to a banquet at which he placed on display a beautiful chest designed to fit only his brother. Jokingly Set offered to give the chest to whoever could fit comfortably inside it, and several tried unsuccessfully. Then Osiris climbed into it, and Set with his conspirators, hastily sealed the chest, weighted it and threw it into the Nile. Isis went in search of the chest, eventually finding it at Byblos where it had been washed ashore. However, a tamarisk tree had grown around it enclosing it completely. The King of Byblos had the tree cut down

their post-mortem days tilling the Elysian fields, whereas the latter is reincarnational or cyclic, the emphasis being on renewal, as Ra passes through the Tuat daily. In fact the *Am-Tuat* was a guide to the otherworld which specified the nature of the beings and entities encountered on the after-death journey, and it contained all the magical formulae necessary for the deceased to pass through the divisions unscathed. The *Book of Gates* on the other hand stresses to a larger extent Osiris' role as lord of the otherworld, and consequently the judgement took on greater significance, for according to the verdict on the scales of *maat*, the deceased would either enter the Elysian fields or be led off to destruction.

However, both works have in common the idea that a knowledge of the post-mortem planes was essential for the living, and in this way, as we have said, the Egyptian books parallel the *Bardo Thodol*. Of course, the *Am-Tuat* and the *Book of Gates* abound with archetypes taking their outward form initially from the Egyptian environment. The huge serpent Apep provides a formidable opponent, and uraei, crocodiles, rivers and deserts, the ibis, hippopotamus and ape were all relevant aspects of the Egyptian world view, enlarged through the imagination to provide deities connoting good and evil. In contra-distinction to the orderly irrigated fields of Osiris, the outer fringes of the otherworld abound with unpredictable, chaotic forms and in the book of *Am-Tuat*, the initiate identifies with Ra because his emergence, by day, is the paramount

---

to be used as a pillar in his palace. Meanwhile Isis entered the royal court in disguise as a maid for Queen Astarte's son. Eventually she revealed her true identity and was presented with the chest, which she took back with her to Egypt. Meanwhile she was pregnant through a magical conception with her dead husband. Osiris hid the coffer in the Delta marshes, but Set accidentally discovered it. Recognizing his dead brother, he tore the body into fourteen pieces and scattered them around the kingdom. Isis went in search of the parts of her husband's body, and found all except the phallus, which had been swallowed by a crab in the Nile. She then embalmed her husband and magically restored him to life, personifying the belief that the immortality of the soul was dependent on the preservation of the body. After a series of subsequent encounters, Isis' son Horus overthrew Set in a number of decisive battles and re-established the dominance of Truth.

certainty. Consequently it provided the only constant factor on which any notion of immortality could be based.

The world of the living was conceived by the ancient Egyptians as surrounded by a chain of mountains. The sun rose by emerging through a hole in the East and sank through a hole in the West. Fairly close to these mountains and beyond them, lay the Tuat. Interestingly it was located not under the ground, but 'parallel with the mountains and . . . on the plane either of the land of Egypt or of the sky above it. . . .'[114] Indeed the duality of light and dark pervades the Egyptian after-death belief—the mountains shielding the Tuat from the light of day and shrouding them in dark and gloom. The light of the Sun god and the magical words of power, *hekau*, provided the means of safe passage. And safe passage was indeed crucial. As Budge writes: 'In all the Books of the otherworld we find pits of fire, abysses of darkness, murderous knives, streams of boiling water, foul stenches, fiery serpents, hideous animal-headed monsters and creatures, and cruel, death-dealing beings of various shapes. . . .'

The Sun was the most central factor in such a Cosmos, the embodiment of creation and vitality. However, all created manifestations existed in the first place because of the *utterance*, because sound had brought them into being. Knowledge of the names of the Tuat deities constituted unquestionable mastery, particularly when the deceased travelled in the boat of the Sun and identified with Ra or Osiris. Osiris had, himself, been installed as overlord of the otherworld by means of words of power obtained from Thoth, the Divine Intelligence.

Both the *Am-Tuat* and *Book of Gates* are self-contained accounts of the underworld as conceived by two distinct sets of religious advocates. The former, which derived from the priests of Amen-Ra at Thebes, stressed the dominance of Amen Ra over all the lords of the regional Tuat: Khenti-Amenti in Abydos, Seker in Memphis, Osiris in Mendes, and Temu-Kheper-Ra in Heliopolis.

[114] Wallis Budge: *The Egyptian Heaven and Hell*, pp. 88–9.

The Osirian development, which gained prominence during the Middle (2160–1580 B.C.) and New Kingdoms (1580–1090 B.C.), outlined a future life based more on good deeds during incarnation than on magic formulae alone. The essence of a man, his heart, is weighed against truth by Anubis the jackal-headed mortuary god. Thoth, the god of wisdom and the divine scribe, records the verdict. Meanwhile the monster Am-nut, a combination of crocodile, lion and hippopotamus, lies in waiting as eater of the condemned. Osiris and forty-two gods in the Hall of Maat witnessed the deceased and his declarations of purity. In both the *Am-Tuat* and *Book of Gates* however, the dead man seeks control. In the *Am-Tuat* it is through hekau, words of power. In the latter it is through a statement of innocence coupled with the proviso that the deceased can penetrate the very existence of the deities in the Hall of two-fold Truth:

'No evil will come to me in this land, in the Hall of two Maats because I know the names of the gods who are of thy company. . . .'

Both books represent, graphically, a progression of the soul, culminating in spiritual renewal. We will consider them separately as symbolic statements concerning the initiation of the deceased through identification with the Sun god. For it is as the master of darkness that the initiate comes forth by day.

The *Am-Tuat* records the progress of the boat of the Sun through the Twelve divisions of the otherworld, that is to say, the twelve hours of night. The Sun god takes the form of the ram, Afu and in the First division three serpents, four man-headed gods, and two hawk-headed gods holding serpents, precede the Tuat boat. The Sun thus embarks upon a journey whereby he gradually transforms himself into the emergent god of the new day.

Second Hour

Here the gods within the boat are the same but two additional deities, Isis and Nephythys lead the way. Four additional boats glide in front of Afu however: the boat of the full moon, the boat of Hathor (Isis): the boat of a Lizard god resting between two sceptres (connoting the jackal gods of South and North) and the boat of the grain god Neper (a form of Osiris, as god of vegetation; grain, herbs and plants). Also present are the bearded god Ast-Netch-t brandishing a phallus knife; Isis the avengeress, and Ibis-aspect of Thoth, some additional corn gods, and a horned animal Amu-aa-, 'eater of the phallus'.

Third Hour

The crew has changed and four mariners, the goddess of the hour, and the hawk-deity bestride the Sun god Afu. Three boats go on ahead; 'the boat which capsizeth'—containing forms of Horus, the 'boat of Rest' containing an Osiris mummy, and a third, containing Osiris with rams' horns and the *upper* portion of his body swathed. Among the other depicted deities are two dog-headed apes, Anubis of Thebes, a bearer of the Eye of Ra, and four mummified forms. They are said to have 'the flesh of their own bodies, and their souls speak over them, and their shadows are united unto them. . . .' Several forms of Osiris are also shown, deities owing their existence to his sustenance, and who hack souls in pieces, and set restraint upon shadows . . . and destroy doomed beings . . . who blazeth with fire. Such is the fate of the foes of the Sun god.

Fourth Hour

The boat of the Sun now proceeds above the kingdom of the Memphite god Seker, an abode enclosed by sand and resting on the backs of sphinxes. The beetle of Khepera emerges above the mound of sand and revivifies Afu-Ra who is led onwards, into 'the midden places'. Several serpent deities, one with semi-human attributes, another with a triple head, hawk wings and human legs constitute barriers to the unworthy. Beneath the boat the cosmic serpent has also undergone a transformation embodying six stars and fourteen human heads, representing the first fourteen days of the month.

Fifth Hour

The Sun boat is now drawn by seven gods and seven goddesses who sing out: 'Ament crieth to thee, O Ra, so that thou may join her, and may go forwards in the sky as the Great One who is in the horizon.' The serpent Ankhaa-Pau is shown, with flames pouring from his mouth. Also present are the goddess Amentit wearing the feather of Maat (truth), five jackal protector gods, eight torturer fire deities, and a hatchet wielding goddess who annihilates the dead. Venus—the five-rayed star beams its light at the gate of entry into the sixth division of the Tuat.

Sixth Hour

Afu-Ra, preceded by Thoth enters into the city of the 'hidden image of Osiris'. Sixteen mummified gods and a five-headed serpent, all symbols of regeneration, enclose Afu and forms of Isis, Osiris and Horus stand nearby. Ape and crocodile deities,—dwellers in the waters of Nu, and the five-headed devourer serpent Am-Khu are also present.

Seventh Hour

Afu, the ram stands beneath a protective snake canopy. Isis meanwhile recites words of power, this knowledge being a prerequisite for presence in the Sun boat. Representations of Tem, Khepera, Ra and Osiris, 'eat their own forms, after the Great God has passed them by'. The lioness goddess Ath and the solar hawk bear the symbols of life, and a huge crocodile, 'the Eye of Ra', stands protectively in front of the twelve goddesses of the hours of night, 'devouring his own form' after the boat has passed through.

Eighth Hour

Afu, protected by serpent Mehen is towed by eight gods who guard the secret images of Horus, (avenger of his father Osiris). Four forms of the solar ram and a number of deities with 'instruments of weaving' are also residents of this division. Nu, the ocean of day, is visible through an open door above a chamber of destruction.

Ninth Hour

Twelve sailor deities transport Afu through the horizon to take up his position in the Eastern Hall of Heaven. Meanwhile four deities—a man headed hawk, a ram-god, a cow-goddess seated on a bowl or basket, and a bearded mummy-deity, provide food—bread and ale—for the gods of the Tuat. Twelve gods, hidden in linen garments at the same time when Osiris hid in the otherworld, are commanded by Horus: 'Uncover your heads . . . unveil your faces . . . and perform the things that must be done for Osiris.' They are represented as having a strongly regenerative function. Meanwhile twelve uraei, mounted on the symbol of weaving—pour forth fire to light the path of Osiris and Horus holds sway over nine bearded gods bearing the symbols of Life.

Tenth Hour

Afu, protected still by Mehen, now holds the symbol of Life in his right hand and the serpent sceptre in his left. A double-headed snake enclosing with its horn-like fold the hawk Heru-Khenti, four disk headed figures, four spearmen, and four bowmen provide his cohorts. They are said to 'spring into life' at the sound of the approaching god, again indicating the vitality of sound in the Egyptian magical religious beliefs. The enemies in the darkness are driven back, by Afu's warriors. Meanwhile the beetle Kheper-Ankh, a form of the emergent sun, pushes along through the sand on one side of the river of the underworld, and two serpents bearing the sun disc are shown facing two young goddesses who make the gesture of silence. Two other solar goddesses, and four with lion's heads are present as well as the Ape god, a form of Thoth, who holds the eye of the sun (Horus) in his hands. Eight gods under the jurisdiction of Horus 'strip the bodies of the dead of their swathings'.

In additional representations ascribed to this division Horus is seen leaning on a staff with a series of male forms, some of whom are submerged, others who float face down, and face up. As an exhortation to overcome old age and decay in the search for new life, Horus says 'Make your way in Nu by means of your legs, and your thighs shall not be in any way impeded . . . for your members shall not perish and your flesh shall not decay, and you shall have dominion over your water.'

Eleventh Hour

The Sun god is still protected by Mehen, but now a sun disc, encircled by a uraeus, sits in the high prow of the boat. The sailors steer the boat into the Eastern horizon. Several entities loyal to Horus are shown, and the serpent Tchet-S with a mummified god upon its back, who casts living ones (stars) to Ra every day prior to swallowing its own form. Horus bearing the solar disc, and leaning on a staff presides over the slaughter of Ra's enemies, and five pits of fire are shown, admirably suited to the purpose: Horus commands: 'Hack into pieces and cut asunder the bodies of the enemies and the members of the dead who have been turned upside down, O my father Osiris . . . and let me come forth.' To his foes he says: 'My father . . . having once been helpless, has smitten you, he has cut up your bodies, he has hacked into pieces your spirits and your souls, and has scattered in pieces your shadows, and has cut into pieces your heads, and you shall never more exist, you shall be overthrown and you shall be cast down headlong into the pits of fire, and you shall not escape therefrom, and you shall not be able to flee from the flames which are in the serpent Set-Heh.'

Twelfth Hour

The Great God now takes up his position and is reborn in the form of Khepera. Nu presides over the birth as he comes forth from the thighs of Nut and enters into the Matet boat, the vessel of the Sun across the oceans of daylight, between sunrise and noon. Mehen still protects the Sun god, but Khepera is shown leading the way. Twelve assistants, creations of the new day, and twelve goddesses guide the boat with the help of the serpent Ka-Em-Ankh-Neteru. Also depicted are twelve goddesses bearing fire-breathing snakes who drive away the darkness, by smiting the chief foe Apep, and twelve other gods who sing the praises of the dawn. Twenty-three further gods uphold the solar disc and follow it to the height of heaven every day:

'Life to thee in all thy majesty. . . . Life to thee, governor of Amentet. . . .'

In the final phase the beetle Khepera emerges from the boat of the Sun god, and the image of Afu, the sun god of the night journey, falls away.

It is clear from this book that spiritual renewal exists as a series of transformations of identity. The initiate, like the Sun god is reborn. His old personality, the Afu, is cast away and the pure spirit comes forth by day. Characteristically the duality of concealment (in the mummy swathings) and re-opening (the new birth) plays an important part. The spirit, protected from the outward forms of chaos emerges from darkness in triumph, in the same way that the anonymity of the magician's cloak, and the barrier of the magical circle shields the magus who would be reborn, from external malicious influences. Several archetypes emerge paralleling the Qabalistic structure, and will be discussed presently.

Meanwhile we can compare the regions of the Tuat as conceived by the more Osirian devotees in the *Book of Gates*, a representation of which is found on the alabaster sarcophagus of King Seti I[115] (1370 B.C.). The 'hours' are distinguished by a series of gateways through which entry must be gained, and safe passage assured.

During the First hour, the Sun is represented as the beetle within the disc, and it prepares to enter the Tuat through a cleft in the mountains of the West. A snake holding its tail inside its mouth protects the disc, and the boat which will carry them is guided by Sa, a form of the divine intelligence. Near the stern and paddles, awaiting instruction stands Heka—personification of magical words of power.

Second Hour

Ra's boat approaches a gateway guarded by the serpent Saa-Set. Sa, riding in the sun boat, commands: 'Open thy door to Ra . . . the hidden abode in is darkness, *so that the transformations of this god may take place.*' The god now becomes a ram-headed man bearing the solar disc above his horns. Thirteen

---

[115] Interestingly, the *Am-Tuat* is inscribed on the walls of the tomb of the same king, indicating a parallel development.

gods of entry ask for the doors of the otherworld to be opened and the aged Tem (the dying Sun god) walks nearby carrying a stick glorifying the Sun god as he enters the Tuat: 'I am the son who proceeds from his father, and I am the father who proceeds from his son.'

Third Hour

This gateway is protected by an outer framework guarded by nine mummy gods. An opening leads to a corridor running between walls barricaded with pointed stakes. At the entrance and exit stand two identical mummified gods who extend their arms to Ra. Flame-spitting serpents are also present to ward off those who do not know the *hekau* of entry.

Further inside lurks one of a number of snake transformations found in the subsequent divisions. The Great God passes through, acclaimed by all, and the gates close after him. Mummified, 'holy gods', an enormous protective snake, and twelve further enshrouded gods who stand waist deep in a lake of boiling water, now come to view. A large ear of wheat grows in front of each of the latter gods, and Ra is said to 'give life to their nostrils', and 'radiance for their darkness' as he passes by. They guard the herbs offered for sacrifice, and are granted in return, immunity from the heat of the boiling lake. Apep, the deadly snake meanwhile is repulsed by words of power and a group of gods, by means of enchantments open the earth to Ra only, closing it against all foes.

Fourth Hour

Similarly guarded externally by nine mummies, the corridor to this division has at each end a mummified form with a uraeus upon his forehead. Inside, as Ra journeys through (past a new snake transformation), are nine mummy shrines, this time lying on their backs. Twelve goddesses of the Horus stand upon land while gods in the waters of the Tuat guide the boat. Twelve bearded gods 'who carry their doubles', twelve 'jackals of life' and ten 'living uraei' can be seen also. As a rite of entry, the jackals allow Ra to immerse himself in the Holy Lake 'where the souls of the dead approach not', and the uraei hurl flames against Ra's enemies. On the other side of the boat, a mummified Osiris can be seen, partly obscured by a mountain, but supported by twenty-four gods who assist Horus towards the resurrection of his father.

Fifth Hour

Guarded as before, this division has jackal-headed gods as watchers over its corridor of entry. Inside, four Egyptians (Reth), four Asiatics (Aāmu), four Libyans (Themehu), and four Negroes (Nehesu) are 'given life' by the Great One.

Sixth Hour

This is an important division of the Tuat since it constitutes none other than the Judgement Hall of Osiris. Twelve mummified 'gods and goddesses of the pylon' present themselves on the outer precincts and two mummified gods Maā-ab, and Sheta-ab (= true of heart and hidden of heart) guard the corridor. The resident gods call upon the god of the boat to 'open the holy doors and unfold the portals of the hidden place'.

Further inside Osiris is visible, seated beneath a canopy housing a row of spears and four horned animals whose heads hang down. A balance is placed before Osiris on which the actions of the deceased during his lifetime will be weighed. At a distance stands Anubis the jackal god, and near to Osiris, the devouring snake who will destroy the wicked. Thoth is not shown.[116] Tem, again portrayed as an elderly man, orders Ra's enemies to be slain.

Meanwhile we see those who enjoy the blessings of Osiris, and who reap grain in the Elysian fields. The 'gods bearing Maat' (truth) are rewarded with offerings and the righteous are given divinely blessed drink and bread.

Seventh Hour

The entrances are similarly portrayed, the gods of the corridor being bearded men with their arms hidden. Sa commands the snake within to open the doorway and it is closed after the admission of the Sun god. Ra, at the same time, protects his rowers through magical power as they tow him

---

[116] He finds representation however in the Papyrus of Ani, which is also Osirian.

towards 'the hidden mountain of the horizon'. Twelve gods whose arms and hands are hidden symbolizing 'the hidden mysteries of the body of Osiris' walk ahead, preceded by eight Neteru-Heti who already begin to see the hidden and secret images. Twelve bearers of forked weapons hold back the serpent fiend Mamu. Also protecting Ra are a monster serpent with twelve human heads and twelve attendants, and the bearded mummy god Qan whose figure is attached to a two-fold rope, grasped by twelve bearded men each guided by a star. This symbolises the capturing of the hours. Also depicted are twelve gods (representing the body of Osiris asleep) upon the serpent Nehep and a number of other gods including a serpent in a circle filled with boiling water. These gods are commanded to come alive: 'Hail O Ye Gods who are over the Tuat . . . and who lie down upon your couches, lift up the flesh of your bodies and gather together your bones, and gird up your members and bring ye into one place your flesh! There is sweet and fresh air for your nostrils. . . . Loose and take off your funeral swathings, untie and remove your wigs, unclose your eyes, and *look ye at the light.*'

Eighth Hour

Again the entrances are similar but the corridor gods are bearded mummies with hands folded upon the breast. Within is the serpent Set-hra and the gate closes as the God passes through. Sa still guides the boat, with Heka obeying at the steering paddles. Four gods tow the boat, headed by an aged god leaning on a staff; 'He who dwelleth in Nu' (a form of Horus?), headed by beings whose names connote 'Bathers', 'Floaters', 'Swimmers' and 'Divers': 'We tow thee along, O Ra, we guide thee, O thou who art at the head of heaven, and thou comest forth to those who are immersed in the waters, and thou shalt make thy way over them.' Those immersed are commanded to look upon Ra: '. . . For it is he who ordereth your destinies.' . . . 'Ye shall have dominion over your waters . . . ye shall pass through the waters of Nu. . . .' Twelve bearded gods give bread and herbs to the deserving souls in the Lake of Fire who are portrayed as bearded human headed hawks with hands raised in adoration. The enemies of Osiris meanwhile are tied and burnt and confront the monster speckled serpent Khet who belches fire, on orders from Horus. 'Ye shall be hacked to pieces, ye shall never more have your being, your souls shall be destroyed and none of you shall live because of what ye have done to my father Osiris: *ye have put his mysteries behind your backs . . . ye have desecrated the hidden things which concern the resting place of the Great One. . . .*'

Ninth Hour

Nine entry gods are shown as previously, with the corridor again guarded by bearded mummies with hands folded upon the breast. Sa commands the gate to be opened to let the light of Ra illumine the darkness. Six bearded magicians, four dog-headed apes and four women 'who work magic by means of knots, for Ra', four spearmen and the ass god, precede the boat. They confront the monster Apep who is defeated by words of power, and the crocodile Shesshes, whom the spearmen stab into pieces.

Meanwhile the souls of Amenti and the followers of Thoth, Horus and Ra are depicted towing Khepri towards the horizon. They cry out . . . 'Come, O Ra, after thy transformations! Appear, appear! . . . The ways of the hidden place are open to thee and the portals which are in the earth are unfolded for thee, the soul which Nut loveth . . . and we will guide thy wings to the mountain. Hail! Enter thou into the East, and make thou thy passage from between the thighs of thy mother.'

Tenth Hour

Sixteen uraei guard the precincts and at the entrances to the corridor stand bearded mummies each holding a knife. Sa commands Dethu to let the god enter, and Heka steers according to his directions.

In front of the boat are *Unti* god of the hour, who holds a star in each hand; four kneeling gods each with a uraeus over the head; three star gods towing a boat containing 'the Face of the Disc'; two serpent deities; a flame-holder and four female 'criers'. Horus-Set is again present. They say: 'We are towing Ra along, and Ra followeth us into Nut. The eye of Horus is about to assist the resurrection of his father, for the Sun god is about to be "united with his face": "Open, thou face of Ra, and let the two eyes of Khti enter into thee." '[117] Again the serpent Apep is stabbed and gashed with knives, and finally fettered by four Setefiu gods who call upon Ra to come forth. Twelve gods prepare to paddle with Ra, and twelve goddesses prepare to tow him across the sky. Ra says to them: 'Take ye the rope, set ye yourselves in position, and pull me, O my followers, into the height of heaven, and lead me along the ways. *My births make you to be born and behold my coming into being maketh you to come into being.*'

Eleventh Hour

The outer precincts of the division take a similar form and a bearded mummy stands guard at each end of the corridor.

Nine knife- and sceptre-bearing gods precede the boat as 'slayers of Apep' (who is in chains). Ra comes forth as an opening is made from the Tuat into Nut (the sky) by the god Amen-Ren-f ('he whose name is hidden').

A series of gods who hold stars and discs giving forth light are depicted and take their place in the body of the sky.

Twelfth Hour

This division represents the final emergence of the Sun god in the light of the new day. Bearded mummies guard the corridor of entry as before, and inside the disc of Tem and the beetle symbol of Khepera are represented. The end of the Tuat has been reached, and the boat of the Sun is about to enter the waters of Nu on a special boat which will ensure that the Sun is not extinguished by the waters of the blue sky. Nu upholds the boat in his hands, and Nut reaches forth to receive the Sun disc which the beetle is rolling towards her. The body of the god is Osiris, reborn, whole and revitalized, symbol of the new day.

[117] The form of Horus 'the enterer', is well known to contemporary Western magic.

Several themes emerge from these two books. The first of these is the duality of concealment and 'coming forth by day'. The deceased, embalmed so that his body would be preserved against decay[118] and fortified for the eventual 're-union' with the soul (as in the Osirian belief) had to emerge from his wrappings to view the light of the new day: (Thus in the *Book of Gates*, division seven: '. . . take off your funeral swathings, untie and remove your wigs, unclose your eyes and look ye at the light. . . .') Those who arrived in the Elysian fields were commanded to throw off their bandages and take possession of their land. In a similar fashion, we note the position of the dwellers in Nu, some of whom float face down, and some face up, the latter absorbing the revitalizing energy of the Sun god as he passes. The *Am-Tuat* includes details of Seker's kingdom and we see the dung beetle rolling the Sun out of concealment in the sand. Khepera is finally reborn as the sun of the dawn in the ocean of Nu and takes his place in the boat of day, ready to traverse the sky.

Arising from the theme of 'coming forth', is the aspect of regeneration. The Sun god gives life to those forms and shapes he passes in the underworld, for light and sound are their very

---

[118] The Egyptian of dynastic times mummified the dead body because they believed that a spiritual body would 'germinate or develop itself' inside it. The parts of the body and soul were as follows:
Khat—the physical body, liable to decay.
Ka—the double, an abstract personality normally dwelling in the tomb of the deceased, but sometimes wandering freely, ghost-like.
Ba—the 'heart' soul, which could take a material or immaterial form, and was sometimes depicted as nourishing the mummified body.
Ab—heart—source of life and both good and evil equating with—conscience—it was vital that the heart should be preserved in the tomb.
Khaibit—the shadow.
Khu—the spiritual body (soul), dwelling in the Sahu. It could never die.
Sekhem—the life force.
Ren—the name—this had to be preserved for a man to exist.
Sahu—The greater spiritual body forming the habitation of the soul.
The celestial body, of the follower of Ra consists of the Ka and Khu which can become a Tet or 'Shining One' who is set like a 'Jewel in the Diadem of the Lord of Spirit and Life made One'. The noumenal essence from which both these derive is the Hammemit which was supposed to revolve around the sun for a period of one hundred and twenty (symbolic) years prior to incarnation.

essence. As he passes by, they dissolve again into darkness until the next passage of the Sun-deity in twenty-four hours time. In a number of instances, we are told that the residents of the Tuat 'eat their own form', that is to say they dissolve 'into nothing' until their next rebirth.

Regeneration is a form of transformation, for even Afu has to be reborn as Khepera. The combinations of gods in the boat of *Am-Tuat* change from division to division. The god receives assistance from Isis, Mehen and so on, as the rite of passage demands. He is towed by his followers on waves of magical sound. His being enters, as it were, the womb of the otherworld, and comes forth transformed. As we have said, the emergence of Ra from the underworld was an observable fact, for he arrived punctually with the dawn. The deceased therefore sought permission to enter his boat, and to ride with him, identifying with him, and feeling the sense of command derived from knowledge of the magical words of power. Osirians believed that they could disembark on reaching the Elysian fields of their resurrected god. The followers of Amen-Ra, who took a more cyclic view, believed they could remain in the blessed company of their god forever, continuing through the eternal sequence of night and day.

To stay near to the god was to ensure sustenance, from the prodigious grain of the Elysian fields, and from meals of wheat cakes and ale. However, in the *Book of Gates* we see that such nourishment is expressed metaphorically. In the sixth division, twelve sickle gods are shown reaping wheat, the ears of which are members of Osiris' own body. Thus, in one sense, Osiris is eaten by his followers. However, Osiris was also the embodiment of maat, and it is clear that his followers are sustained by truth and 'will exist as Truth for ever'.

Those who had turned away from Osiris, and had 'put his mysteries behind their backs' following a life of wickedness and ignorance were damned forever. For the light of day could only benefit those worthy to receive it. The foes of Osiris would be scorched inexorably from existence.

THE PATH OF THE CHAMELEON

Wallis Budge writes:

'The shadows, souls and bodies of those who were without food in the Tuat were, together with the fiends and monsters which opposed the progress of the Sun god, destroyed by fire each day, utterly and finally; but each day brought its own supply of the enemies of Ra, and of the dead, and the beings which were consumed in the pits of fire one day were not the *same*, though they belonged to the *same classes* as those which had been burnt up the day before.'[119]

The self-contained *Am-Tuat* and *Book of Gates* provide probably the most graphic accounts of an after-death belief in the ancient world. Paradoxically, though, the compilation of prayers, hymns and funerary orations known as *The Egyptian Book of the Dead* is better known. This work brings together many of the more fragmentary and less complete works like the notable *Papyrus of Ani*, the *Papyrus of Nebseni*, the *Papyrus of Nu* and the *Book of Breathings*.

Many of the themes discussed above are present here also, among them the power of the utterance, the concept of transformation and the identification of the limbs of the body with various gods.

The names of the gods of the seven Arits or mansions of Osiris had to be known by heart, and those of the forty-two gods of the twenty-one pylons in the Elysian fields.[120] The address for the first pylon is as follows:

'I have made my way. I know you and I know your name, and I know the god who guardeth you. Lady of tremblings, with lofty walls, the sovereign Lady, the mistress of destruction who setteth in order the words which drive back the whirlwind and the storm, who delivereth from destruction him that travelleth along the way is thy name. The name of thy doorkeeper is Neri.'

In both the *Papyrus of Nebseni* and that of *Ani* it is evident that the so-called ceremony of the 'Opening of the Mouth' refers to

---

[119] Wallis Budge: *The Egyptian Heaven and Hell* p. 199.
[120] The Sekhet-Aaru, part of the domain of Osiris.

the ability to utter sacred names and to 'speak in the presence of Osiris'. Performed by a priest for the benefit of the dead, the ceremony had as its basis the mythological axiom that Thoth had created the world by means of a sacred word, and had provided Isis with the magical formulae necessary for Osiris' resurrection, and that accordingly the dead person would need to speak in order to be reborn. In Chapter XXII, of the *Papyrus of Ani*, the scribe announces: 'I rise out of the egg into the hidden land. May my mouth be given unto me that I may speak . . . in the presence of the Great God, the Lord of the Tuat . . .' and further on, 'Moreover may Thoth, being filled and furnished with charms, come and loose my bandages, even the bandages of Set[101] which fetter my mouth, and may the god Tem hurl them at those who would fetter me with them and drive them back. May my mouth be opened, may my mouth be unclosed by Shu with (the) iron knife . . . (with which) he opened the mouth of the gods.'

If knowledge of hekau, provided safe passage in the Tuat, the identification between parts of the human body and certain major deities constituted additional mastery, by the act of 'containment'. In the *Papyrus of Nu*, we read: 'My hair is the hair of Nu. My face is the face of the Disc. My eyes are the eyes of Hathor . . . my neck is the neck of the divine goddess Isis . . . my phallus is the phallus of Osiris, my hips and legs are those of Nut . . . my feet are the feet of Ptah. . . . The god Thoth shieldeth my body . . . and I am Ra day by day. . . .'

In Chapter LXVIII, 'Of coming forth by day' from the *Papyrus of Nu*, the 'triumphant Nu' says: 'I have gained the mastery over my heart; I have gained the mastery over my breast; I have gained the mastery over my mouth . . . I have gained the mastery over all the things which were ordered to be done for me upon earth and in the otherworld. . . .'

The deceased was thus transformed: 'I am the Lord of transformations for I have the transformations of every god, and

[101] . . . the murderer of Osiris and antagonist of Horus.

they go round about in me.'[122] In his final form he would rise as the 'hawk of gold' or bennu bird, the Egyptian equivalent of the phoenix, and symbol of spiritual rebirth: 'I have risen, I have risen like the mighty hawk (of gold) that cometh forth from the egg . . . I have come from the interior of the Sektet boat and my heart hath been brought unto me from the mountain of the east . . . I have risen and have gathered myself together like the beautiful hawk of gold which hath the head of a bennu bird, and Ra entereth in day by day to hearken unto my words. . . .'

[122] Wallis Budge: *The Egyptian Book of the Dead.* Routledge & Kegan Paul, London. Second edition 8th impression, 1960, Ch. CLXXIX from the Papyrus of Nu.

CHAPTER TWO

Graeco-Roman Shamans and Journeys to the Underworld

The traditions of the Greeks and Romans continued the idea of the connection between the underworld of death and the possibility of spiritual rebirth. In Homer, Plato, Ovid, Pindar, Virgil, Statius, Proclus, and in the account of shamans or ecstatics like Aristeas of Proconnesus, we find repeatedly the notion that one can go down into the bowels of the earth, and ascend to the light of purity beyond Olympus. Also present is a strong emphasis on cycles of rebirth, the aim of the initiate being to become successively purer through lessons learned in incarnation.

Ovid, in *Metamorphoses* XV writes:

'O race of men, stunned with the chilling fear of death, why do you dread the Styx, the shades and empty names . . . our souls are deathless . . . the spirit wanders, comes now here, now there, and occupies whatever frame it pleases. . . . And as the pliant wax is stamped with new designs, does not remain as it was before nor keep the same form long, but is still the selfsame wax, so do I teach that the soul is ever the same, though it passes into ever-changing bodies. . . . All things are in a state of flux, and everything is brought into being with a changing nature. Time itself flows on in constant motion, just like a river. . . .'

However, rebirth has always had a two-fold meaning. It signifies, most obviously, a succession of physical existences, but it also has a profound second emphasis as spiritual renewal in the single life of the individual. In the same way that the Egyptians identified with Ra in his transformations through the darkness of the Tuat, and his 'coming forth by day' so too, did the accounts of the descent into the underworld, current in Graeco-Roman mythology offer the possibility of 'emergence'. It has been said that entry into a cave, often the doorway to Hades, represents a 'change of state' and this is quite true. The hero who ventured down past the Styx, who witnessed first hand the fate of the wicked and the dwellings of the blessed, and who encountered gods, and strange phantastic forms, was indeed a man of knowledge.

Such mythical visits to the underworld are sure to have occurred in a wide range of ancient cultures. Gilgamish, hero of the great epic, went westwards to the mountain Mashu, behind which the sun set. He encountered two scorpion deities guarding the entrance leading upward to heaven and down to Arullu, the underworld. As in the Egyptian account, Gilgamish crosses through the Sea of Death 'which only Shamash (the Sun) could cross', reaching the place of new day, a garden of the gods where the cosmic tree was growing.

E. R. Dodds, and the Swiss scholar Meuli, believe that the Greeks may have come into contact with shamanistic ethnic cultures in Scythia and Thrace. A shaman, it must be remembered, is one who makes the journey of the soul down into the underworld, or through the skies of heaven, in a form suitable for his purpose. The siberians used a number of bird and animal forms, and the legendary Greek Shaman Aristeas, as we shall see, 'went forth' in the form of a raven.

The entry to the underworld is usually in the west, the place of the setting sun. Brandon stresses that the burial of the dead beneath the ground accounts for the fact that traditionally 'the habitat of the dead was Subterranean'.[123] Eventually, however, the Greeks were able to accommodate the belief that the afterworld also included the atmosphere, and the regions of the stars. 'Even heaven and hell are presently located in the air,' writes Jackson Knight. 'The supreme attainment is very high,

---

[123] S.G.F. Brandon: *The Judgment of the Dead*. Weidenfeld and Nicolson, London, 1967, p. 2.

with gods near or on the sun. Or the moon is the lower sphere of the hereafter, the sun the higher, and the space between intermediate—a rudimentary heaven, hell, and purgatory.'[124]

A myth connected with this type of differentiation is that of Castor and Polydeuces (Pollux), the two half brothers, the first mortal, the second immortal and son of Zeus. After the death of Castor in war, which portended separate destinies, Polydeuces appealed to his father so that their fates could be 'levelled': each would spend half his time 'beneath the earth, and half in the golden abodes of heaven'. It is clear from the account in Pindar's *Odes* that Castor and Polydeuces represent the sun and moon, which for half their time are hidden from earth.

In the time of Homer it was believed to be almost impossible for even a very notable hero to become a god, but some four hundred years later, every neophyte of the Orphic mysteries was told: 'You shall be a god instead of a mortal.'

The Greek mystery religions, which extended their influence to Rome, were in fact elaborate systems of initiation for transforming man out of his narrow physical existence into a universe filled with mystic splendour. The Orphics referred to the body as a tomb, indicating what freedom lay in the release of the spirit, and in a knowledge of 'what to do and say after death'. The soul of an initiate would undergo reincarnations and in the end emerge as a pure spirit living in heaven among the stars. Olympus becomes a heaven beyond the sky, far removed from its early form as a mountain.

In the Eleusinian mysteries, which we have mentioned earlier in connection with Demeter and Persephone, the symbolism of the regenerated productivity of the earth, as a system of cycles had profound metaphorical parallels with the fate of man. In the rites of Eleusis (a name having a common origin with Elysion—the realm of the blessed), the initiates that had passed through a period of fasting and the preliminary mysteries at Agrai, drank, from the kykeon, a sacred potion made of barley,

[124] W. F. Jackson Knight: *Elysion*. Rider, London, 1970, p. 62.

mint and water. This stimulatory beverage assisted the initiate in experiencing as a transcendental reality the beatific vision of the emergent Persephone.[125] Kerenyi notes that the return of Persephone from Hades offered man a 'world . . . full of food and hope'.[126] Her offspring Dionysus came to symbolize 'all natural life and vigour in the fullest and widest sense'.[127] Persephone's happy second marriage, to Eubouleus, harbinger of perfection in the world, also indicated a new harmony. The partakers of the sacrament in the Telestrion, now understood that 'men might die more confidently after having lived better'.[128] Rohde says: 'To those who share in the Eleusinian worship a privileged fate is promised after death, but even in his lifetime . . . he is highly blessed whom the two goddesses love: they send him Ploutos, the giver of good things, to be a beloved partner of his hearth and home.'

On the other hand, whosoever honours not Kore, the queen of the lower world, with gifts and sacrifice, shall do penance everlastingly . . . the mysteries promised immortality. Demeter is the earth, Kore—Persephone the daughter, the seed of corn. The rape and return of Kore mean the sowing of the seed in the earth and the rise of the young grain from beneath the soil. . . . In some way or other the Mystai must have had revealed to them the real meaning of the 'nature symbolism'. They are supposed to have learnt that the fate of the seed of corn, represented by Persephone, its disappearance beneath the earth and eventual rebirth, is an image of the fate of the human soul, which also disappears that it may live again.[129]

---

[125] Dr. Albert Hofmann the synthesizer of L.S.D., has provided Kerenyi with a note to the effect that fasting coupled with 'spiritual preparations' could in themselves have produced hallucinatory effects. Kerenyi adds that the 'mint' component of the liquid drink which was sipped from the Kykeon, could have contained aromatic Oleum Pulegii and this would certainly have heightened any transcendental sensations. Rohde notes, in *Psyche* (p. 273), that the Scythians, and the Dionysians of Thrace also opened the doors of the unconscious by intoxicating themselves with hashish.
[126] C. Kerenyi: *Eleusis*, Routledge & Kegan Paul, London, 1967, p. 169.
[127] E. Rohde: *Psyche*. Kegan Paul, Trench, Trubner, London 1925, p. 285.
[128] C. Kerenyi: *Eleusis*, p. 174.
[129] E. Rohde: *Psyche*, pp. 219, 223–4.

GRAECO-ROMAN SHAMANS, UNDERWORLD JOURNEYS

Now the Orphic and Dionysian religions were characteristically ecstatic. According to Rohde: 'The "ekstasis", the temporary *alienato mentis* of the Dionysiac cult was not thought of as a vain purposeless wandering in a region of pure delusion, but as a hieromania, a sacred madness in which the soul, leaving the body, winged its way to vision with the god.'[130] Dionysus, or Bacchus as he came to be identified—the god of wines and vegetation 'and the whole of Nature's rich and flourishing growth', was as Kerenyi has shown, also a resident of the underworld. For the living to meet him, they had to journey, as a shaman in the 'soul-body', down into the regions where normally only the dead, as disembodied souls, would venture.

E. R. Dodds points out that Orpheus, founder of the other great mystery school, was also a shaman, and 'like certain legendary figures in Siberia . . . (could) by his music summon birds and beasts to listen to him. Like shamans everywhere, he pays a visit to the underworld, and his motive is one very common among shamans—to recover a stolen soul. Finally his magical self lives on as a singing head, which continues to give oracles for many years after his death.'[131]

These eschatological myths of the underworld are also found in the Roman Literature, a fine example occurring in Vergil's *Aeneid VI*. The Trojans come to a land in the west looking for a 'new city of the gods'. Aeneas lands at Cumae, near Naples, and comes to the entrance to the world of the dead, over-lorded by Apollo and Diana (Sun and Moon). A sibyl guards the Temple of Apollo and the entrance to the cave. Meanwhile Aeneas deciphers the labyrinth on the gates of the Temple. After making sacrifices and receiving prophecies from the sibyl, Aeneas enters the underworld in search of the 'golden bough' which will ensure his safe passage. He crosses the Styx in the ferry of Charon, encounters evil spirits and lost colleagues and

---
[130] E. Rohde: *Psyche*, p. 259.
[131] E. R. Dodds: *The Greeks and the Irrational*. University of California, 1951, p. 147.

hears of the fate of the wicked in the depths of Tartarus. Then he finds his father, Anchises, in Elysium, a country whose walls are built by the Cyclops. Anchises shows him a vision of Roman history, and explains certain secrets of the universe, and Aeneas emerges through the ivory gate of sleep, a *renewed* man.[132] 'After the great experience, there is a change in Aeneas, he is firmer, with a stronger faith.'

Francis Cornford, the noted Platonic Scholar, believes that this myth is strongly in the Greek tradition: Like the otherworld references of Pindar, the sixth *Aeneid* points 'to a common source which may have been an Orphic apocalypse, a descent of Orpheus into Hades'.[133] It also shares a number of significant features—the divine origin of the soul; the torments of the wicked and the happiness of the just in the interval between incarnations, the Elysian meadow and the waters of the underworld—with the important Myth of Er, mentioned in Book X of Plato's *Republic*. Cornford summarizes Plato's cosmology:

Plato's universe is spherical. At the circumference the fixed stars revolve; inside the sphere are the seven planets (including sun and moon). Souls do not see the universe itself, but a model, resembling a spindle on an axis, resting on the knees of necessity. The mechanism is turned by the Fates, Clotho (the Spinner), Lachesis (she who allots), and Atropos (the inflexible). 'Sirens sing eight notes at consonant intervals forming the structure of a scale (harmonia) which represents the Pythagorean "music of the spheres". All this imagery is of course, mythical and symbolic. The underlying doctrine is that in human life there is an element of necessity or chance, but also an element of free choice, which makes us, and not Heaven, responsible for the good and evil in our lives.'[134]

The valiant Er is killed in battle. When the dead are taken

---

[132] W. F. Jackson Knight: Vergil: Epic and Anthropology. George Allen & Unwin, London, 1967, p. 143.
[133] F. M. Cornford: *Plato's Republic*. Clarendon Press, Oxford, pp. 340-1.
[134] F. M. Cornford: *Plato's Republic*, p. 342.

for burial, his body is found undecayed. His body is carried home, and after two days, placed on the funeral pyre. He now comes to life and describes what he has seen 'in the other world':

> 'When his soul left its body, it firstly came to a place where there were two openings side by side in the earth, and opposite them two others in the sky above. Between them sat Judges who after each sentence given, bade the just take the way to the right upwards through the sky, first binding on them in front tokens signifying the judgement passed upon them. The unjust were commanded to take the downward road to the left, and these bore evidence of all their deeds fastened on their backs. Er is told to observe everything that occurs and carry the knowledge back to earth. He sees "souls coming up out of the earth travel-stained and dusty, or down from the sky clean and bright" who meet to discuss their travels in the Meadow. Some had journeyed under the earth for a thousand years, others had enjoyed the inconceivable beauty of heaven. All sinners paid in torments ten times as oppressive as the misdeed committed on earth. After seven days, the company leaves the Meadow and journeys onwards. On the fourth day, they come to a straight shaft of light, like a pillar, stretching from above throughout heaven and earth, more like a rainbow than anything else, but brighter and purer. . . . There, at the middle of the light, they (see) stretching from heaven the extremities of its chains, for this light binds the heavens, holding together all the revolving firmament. . . . And from the extremities (stretches) the Spindle of Necessity, by means of which all the circles revolve.'

There are eight whorls 'set one within the other'. The first and outermost is the broadest, the Fixed Stars. The next in order of *broadth* are the sixth, (Venus), the fourth, (Mars), the eighth (Moon), seventh (Sun); fifth (Mercury) third (Jupiter) and the second (Saturn). The Sun is the brightest and gives light to the Moon.

'The Spindle turned on the Knees of Necessity. Upon each of its circles stood a Siren, who carried round with its movement, uttering a single sound on one note, so that all the eight made up the concords of a single scale. Round about, at equal distances, were seated, each upon a throne, the three daughters of Necessity, the Fates, robed in white with garlands on their heads, Lachesis, Clotho and Atropos, chanting to the Siren's music, Lachesis of things past, Clotho of the present, and Atropos of things to come. . . .'

Newly-deceased souls were required to go before Lachesis where an interpreter holding lots representing different types of lives, scattered them before the newcomers—each to choose. All types of lives, beneficent and tyrannical, human and animal, were included in the lots. The purpose, according to Plato 'to distinguish the good life from the evil, and always and everywhere to choose the best within (one's) reach'. This entails following a *middle* way 'that avoids extremes' if the individual is to find 'the greatest happiness'. For he should not be dazzled by wealth or the promise of power in the next incarnation to come.

'It was indeed, said Er, a sight worth seeing, how the souls severally chose their lives—a sight to move pity and laughter and astonishment; for the choice was mostly governed by the habits of their former life.' He saw one soul choosing the life of a swan; this had once been the soul of Orpheus, which so hated all womankind because of his death at their hands that it would not consent to be born of woman (Orpheus was torn to pieces by the Maenads, female worshippers of Dionysus). . . . The soul which drew the twentieth lot took a lion's life; this had been Ajax, the son of Telemon, who shrank from being born as a man, remembering the judgement concerning the arms of Achilles. (For after Achilles' death Ajax and Odysseus fought for the trophy of his arms. Ajax was defeated and committed suicide). Similarly, Agamemnon takes the life of an eagle, because he despises mankind, and Atalanta wishes to become an athlete, and to win great honours. The last choice falls to Odysseus himself, who chooses a life of obscurity—neglected by all the others.

When the souls have chosen their lives, they pass on to Lachesis who gives 'each into the charge of the guardian genius he had chosen, to escort him through life and fulfil his choice'.

> 'The genius led the soul first to Clotho, under her hand as it turned the Whirling Spindle, thus ratifying the portion which the man had chosen when his lot was cast. And, after touching her, he led it next to the spinning of Atropos, thus making the thread of destiny irreversible. Thence, without looking back, he passed under the throne of Necessity. And when he and all the rest had passed beyond the throne, they journeyed together to the Plain of Lethe through terrible stifling heat; for the plain is bare of trees and of all plants that grow on the earth. When evening came, they encamped beside the River of Unmindfulness, whose water no vessel can hold. All are required to drink a certain measure of this water . . . every man as he drinks forgets everything.'

Er does not drink from the River, and opens his eyes on the funeral pyre, graphically aware of all that has happened to him.

Er, like Aeneas, is an archetypal shaman, for he journeys into the underworld and returns, filled with the knowledge of his experience.

The Greeks and Romans knew this phenomenon as the journey of the soul, and referred to it as 'riding through the air in the god's chariot'. Contemporary theurgic magic knows it as astral projection, and investigators of extra-sensory perception, like Celia Green, Charles Tart and Robert Crookall, know it as the 'ecsomatic' or 'out-of-the-body' experience.

We find lucid accounts of such phenomena in the classical literature, one of them by Proclus referring to an occasion at which Aristotle was present.

'He struck the boy with the wand, drew out his soul, and so to speak, guided it from the body with the wand, afterwards showing that the body was all the time lying motionless and undamaged, and that it remained insensible to the blows, like a corpse. The soul had meanwhile departed from the body.

'After having been led back to the body with the help of the wand, (and) after entering, it told all (what it had seen). This experiment convinced all the other spectators as well as Aristotle that the soul could separate itself from the body.'[135]

Pliny in his *Naturalis Historia VII* writes:

'The soul of Hermotimus of Clazomenae would leave his body, range abroad and report distant happenings unknowable except to an eye-witness, while his body itself would be betwixt life and death. . . .'

One of the most famous cases however was that of Aristeas of Proconnesus, who is mentioned by Herodotus, Pliny, Suidas and Maximus of Tyre. Pliny writes that 'the soul of Aristeas was seen flying from his mouth . . . in the form of a raven,'[136] and Maximus has this account:

'There was a man of Proconnesus whose body would lie alive, yes, but with only the dimmest flicker of life and in a state very near to death; while his soul would issue from it and wander in the sky like a bird, surveying all beneath, land, sea, rivers, cities, nations of mankind and occurrences and creatures of all sorts.

---

[135] Proclus: In *Rempubalican II*, quoting Clerchus, a follower of Aristotle. The question of the dualism of mind and body has been a central one throughout the history of philosophy, and continues to raise its head, particularly as the result of extra-sensory perception. The out-of-the-body experience, recorded extensively in medical and scientific records, tends of course to support it.

John Beloff in *The Existence of Mind* (MacGibbon & Kee, London 1962) notes that science has replaced philosophy as the sole arbiter of all genuine knowledge (p. 13). If this is so, dualism could become increasingly acceptable again. It tends, however, as Beloff points out, to run counter to Behaviouristic models which stress organic function rather than consciousness, a key factor in the debate. Thus Idealism, the School of Plato, 'makes Mind primary and the Body a mere vehicle through which it expresses itself', whereas the materialistic view 'makes the Body and its workings primary and Mind a mere reflection of them in consciousness' (p. 212). Both Aldous Huxley and Bergson stressed that the brain was not productive, as the Behaviourists hold, but *eliminative*. The mind is seen as potentially unlimited. However, attention is given only to the retention of knowledge 'of more or less immediate practical concern to the organism in its struggle for existence'.

Beloff notes that 'in the long run the case for dualism is likely to stand or fall with the success or failure of parapsychology' (p. 258). However, the pragmatic, systematic exploration of the unconscious mind using techniques of western high magic could be equally, if not more instructive. (See also *Appendix A* on Reincarnation.)

[136] Pliny: *Naturalis Historia VII*. It is fruitful to compare this account with the statements of the present day Mexican shaman Don Juan Matus who believes that the consciousness should be transformed into the 'image' or vehicle of a crow. See Carlos Castaneda: *The Teachings of Don Juan* (Penguin Books 1970, p. 164). Follow-up works include *A Separate Reality* (1971) and *Journey to Ixtlan* (1972).

Then, returning into and raising up its body, which it treated like an instrument it would relate the various things it had seen and heard in various places.'[137]

Proconnesus is an island in the sea of Marmara. Aristeas is said to have 'died' suddenly, and to have gone on a shamanistic journey, after which an account was written—the *Arimaspea*. Herodotus mentions in his Historiae IV that Aristeas was in a fuller's shop at the time of his collapse, and that the owner closed the shop while he went off to tell Aristeas' kindred what had happened:

> 'The report of the death had just spread through the town, when a certain Cyzicenian (i.e. a dweller of Cyzicus) lately arrived from Artace contradicted the rumour, affirming that he had met Aristeas on the road to Cyzicus and had spoken with him. This man, therefore, strenuously denied the rumour; the relations however proceeded to the fuller's shop with all things necessary for the funeral, intending to carry the body away. But on the shop being opened, no Aristeas was found either dead or alive. Six years afterwards he reappeared, they told me, in Proconnesus, and composed the poem known as the *Arimaspea* after which he disappeared a second time.'

In the *Arimaspea*, which survives as fragments, Aristeas, possessed by Apollo journeys beyond Scythia to the neighbouring river dwellers, the Issedonians, with whom he stays for some time. They tell him about an icy snow-capped mountain range, home of the freezing wind of Boreas, and of the land between these mountains, and their own river rich in gold. This treasure is guarded by griffins until one-eyed hairy savages, the Arimaspi, steal it from them. According to additional details supplied by Maximus, 'the limit of the journey was the country of the Hyperboreans'. Aristeas would tell 'how he thus obtained a successive view of all usages customary and political, at varying landscapes and climates, of inroads of the sea and outpourings of rivers; and how his soul then had *a much clearer view of heaven than from below on earth*' (Philosophumena XXXVIII).

[137] Maximus of Tyre: *Philosophomena* X (II).

Bolton, in his book on Aristeas, notes the remarkable accuracy of the ethnographic details presented in the *Arimaspea*, which was compiled at a time (between 675 B.C. and 465 B.C.) when such knowledge was marginal. Aristeas, he writes, 'brought back with him an essentially true account of the nomadic peoples beyond the Black Sea',[138] and does not appear to have borrowed his information from any other writers. Further on, Bolton acknowledges the shamanistic viewpoint of Alfoldi, Meuli, and others, but declines to accept it himself because he finds it difficult to accommodate both authentic and imaginative components as part of the shamanistic process. The Scyths and Issedonians are clearly real people, but the one-eyed Arimaspi do not appear to be. (They tend rather to parallel the peculiar one-legged people Swedenborg observed as visionary inhabitants of the moon).

As we have seen earlier, out-of-the-body experiences can provide accurate three-dimensional information about one's surroundings, as if seen from another vantage point. But such 'projection' can also lead to visionary experiences. Aristeas seems to have undergone both. His initial ecsomatic accounts are accurate, but they are soon tinged with elements of phantasy. It is not surprising that, since Aristeas is 'possessed by Apollo', he encounters the griffins, sacred to that very god, and who guard the gold, symbolic of the Sun. Apollo enjoys the company of the Hyperboreans, those beyond the cold slopes of the freezing mountains, and it is in such a 'heaven' that Aristeas' soul-body finds its 'limit', as Maximus tells us. Like the followers of Ra, who similarly journey beyond the mountains in the Tuat, Aristeas identifies as one of the company of the god. Like the followers of the emergent Sun he reappears. Unlike them he is alive prior to undertaking the visionary journey and so he is able to reaffirm his physical existence subsequently and to provide an account of what has occurred. *The Egyptian Books of the Dead*, while applicable to the living, are expressed only as journals of the deceased. Bolton finds

[138] J. D. P. Bolton: *Aristeas of Proconnesus*. Clarendon Press, Oxford, 1962, p. 3.

difficulty in accounting for the one-eyed hairy hoarders of the gold, and suggests that they might have been Mongols. The Arimaspi may indeed have been inspired by such people but they are predominantly mythical within the account of Aristeas. They rather resemble Alberich's gold-hoarding gnomes of Wagner's *Rhinegold*, and we are reminded that gnomes are elementals of the earth, and liable to appear on visionary encounters in the trance state.

Aristeas provides us with a very remarkable case because he is 'reborn' in a double sense. He reappears after his body has apparently 'died'—which we understand as an ecsomatic experience, and he returns from the lofty company of the Hyperboreans, vanguard of Apollo. Insofar as we are inclined to identify the resurrected Christ with Osiris-Apollo, who parallels him in many ways, it is interesting to note that the griffin is also a symbol of Christ. We quote Borges: 'In Canto XXIX of the *Purgatorio*, Dante has a vision of a triumphal chariot (the Church) drawn by a Griffon; its eagle portion is golden, its lion portion white mixed with red in order to signify—according to the commentaries—Christ's human nature . . . the commentators are recalling the description of the beloved in the Song of Solomon (V:10–11) "My beloved is white and ruddy. . . . His head is as the most fine gold".'[139]

Finally, it is perhaps not inappropriate to note that many features of the tale of Aristeas—namely the man from Cyzicus who 'saw' him on the road; the missing body in the sealed shop; and the subsequent return to the same place after an interval of time spent in ascent to 'heaven'—parallel the mythology associated with Christ's resurrection and predate it by approximately five hundred years.

[139] Jorge Luis Borges. *The Book of Imaginary Beings*. Discus/Avon Books, New York 1969, p. 116.

CHAPTER THREE

The Chaldean Oracles

The Egyptian and Graeco-Roman cultures have provided Western magic, as we have seen, with an elaborate after-death mythos, coupled with notable tales of the shamanistic 'journey of the soul'. From such eschatology it is possible to construct a viable system for the controlled expansion of consciousness. However, we are indeed fortunate that two such formulations were in fact evolved in antiquity, long prior to the operation of modern pragmatic occult orders like the Golden Dawn. I refer to the Neoplatonic Chaldean Oracles, for whose compilation and presentation in an English translation we must be grateful to Hans Lewy,[140] and to the Qabalah with its profoundly universal symbol of the Tree of Life. The Gnostic fragments would undoubtedly have constituted a workable system too, had they not been ruthlessly suppressed as heretical tracts by the fathers of the early Christian Church.

The *Chaldean Oracles* grew out of Greek (and Persian)[141] culture and represent the philosophical achievement of three major figures, Julian the Chaldean; Julian the Theurgist, his son, and the Neoplatonist Iamblichus whom Emperor Julian regarded as a finer intellect than Plato. Julian the younger, who is believed to have authored the major part of the collected *Oracles* lived during the time of Trajan, Hadrian and Marcus

---

[140] Hans Lewy: *Chaldean Oracles and Theurgy*. De L'Institut Francais D'Archeologie Orientale, Cairo, 1956.

[141] The important 'Chaldean' deity Aion, was a form of Zurvan, the Persian god of Time, introduced into the world of the Neoplatonists by Mithraism.

Aurelius. Iamblichus is thought to have lived between 250 and *circa* A.D. 325 The combined Oracles constitute 'the doctrines which the gods disclosed to the two Julians', Apollo and the goddess Hecate, allegedly providing paramount inspiration.

Porphyry, who brought the tracts to the attention of the Neoplatonists, approximately a hundred years after they were written, says that the true divine source of these writings could hardly be known because the supreme God, the 'noetic Primordial Fire', did not reveal his nature.

Porphyry presents a structure of the manifested universe in his own work *On the Philosophy of the Oracles*. According to Porphyry, the peak of creation is resident in the Father of the gods—'Mystes', who generates the First Intellect, the 'Vigour of Strength' (feminine—Mother), and who in turn produces Ideas forming the second intellect (masculine—Son). Outside the triad permeates an 'unbounded mobile fire, self-manifest, engendered without birth, incorporeal and immaterial . . .' the infinite Aion. 'Therefrom fires go forth in a circle round the Olympus.'

Mystes, the Primordial Fire, the 'Form within Forms' constitutes the Monad; the second manifestation is the great Mother, the 'womb that contains everything', and the Son is their divine offspring.

Beneath the Supernal triad we find four emanations: Soul, Spirit, Harmony, and Number, as aspects of the Cosmic Soul (Hecate). Porphyry's system is then, one of a Seven-fold universe.

The theurgists as a group sought transcendental union with the gods not as a process of intellect, but as an ascension of the soul, in much the same way as their Platonic and Orphic forebears. In their ritual oracles, they sought to bring the gods within their group, and the deity would descend, on invocation, into the 'recipient', the medium for the oracle. Apollo and Hecate feature strongly in the *Oracles*, the Supernal triad being somewhat remote Porphyry provides an account of the oracle of Apollo filling the sibyl:

'The stream separating from the Splendour of Phoebus (Apollo-Helios) on high, and enveloped in the sonorous breath of pure air, falls enchanted by songs and by ineffable words about the heads of the blameless recipient . . . it produces out of the mortal flute a lovely song. . . .'[142]

'Blameless' in this connotation apparently signifies ritual purity for the Neoplatonist, like the Orphics, believed that the 'tomb' of the body had to be sanctified before it could give forth a soul which could find mystical union with a god.

Beneath the Supernals lay the region of Hecate. The noetic, or Supernal deities subsisted in her all-encompassing fire, and she was a direct emanation of the First Intellect, the Great Mother in another form. Normally she was identified with the Moon, counterposed to the Sun—the abode of Apollo and symbol of Truth. However, she was also said to be surrounded with understanding (Hermes/Mercury) and linked with Persephone and Artemis. One non-Chaldean oracle links Hecate, Artemis and Persephone as a unified triad over ether, air and earth. The Chaldean Oracles proper, however, represent Hecate as a fearsome deity who does not dwell on the Moon itself, but descends in fire when invoked, ready to plague with demonic spirits the Theurgist who is ritually impure.

The Theurgists, like the Egyptians laid great emphasis on the power of the utterance and guarded respectfully their knowledge of the 'ineffable names', for these names were strong enough to lure and 'bind', and to cause the god to 'descend'. Such 'binding' of the deity was expressed as the onslaught of the Theurgist armoured with a luminous body,[143] and holding as his weapons the magical words of power. Nevertheless the Theurgists differed from the practitioners of sorcery (the goetic art), whom they despised, insofar as they did not threaten, but merely 'persuaded' the invoked forces. And during 'elevation', that is to say, the mystical ascent of

---

[142] Quoted in Hans Lewy: *Chaldean Oracles and Theurgy*, p. 43.

[143] The mystical ascent is an 'ecsomatic' or 'out-of-the-body' experience. Thus the luminous body is the same as the familiar 'body of light' of western magicians, used for ventures on the astral planes.

consciousness, the 'soul' of the initiate was believed to unite with a ray sent towards him from the Sun.

Porphyry's Neoplatonic system is essentially the same as that of the Chaldean Oracles proper which Lewy has reconstructed from a body of fragments contained in the writings of Iamblichus, Proclus and Damascius. Regrettably only three of the original Oracles are quoted in full. Nevertheless the structure which emerges is as follows:

FIRST EMANATION: SUPREME BEING (Male)
This is the All-Father; Father of men and gods, Supreme King of the Blessed, all these terms being purely appellations for the intrinsically indescribable. Composed of Spiritual Fire, 'uniquely Transcendent, Silent', and resident above the seven planets and fixed stars, His action unfolds through his intermediaries. These are said to constitute his *faculties* in a system that is essentially monotheistic: 'All things descent from one Fire.'

SECOND EMANATION: INTELLECT, WILL, POWER (Female)
   and
THIRD EMANATION: IDEAS (Male)
The Second Emanation is also called the 'Artisan', and fashions the Cosmos in the likeness of the 'imperishable form' transmitted by the Father. From the Mother, comes forth the Son, in the form of Ideas that mould the universe like a hammersmith. He is thus the Demiurge, and parallels Zeus, hurler of thunderbolts.

FOURTH EMANATION: WORLD SOUL (Female)
Personified by Hecate and Psyche, she is a direct creation of the Father, and is filled with Intellect and Power. Immortal, 'Mistress of Life' she pours forth from her right hip Soul (Light, Fire, Ether and the Worlds) and from her left Virtue, maintaining her virginity, or purity. Goddess of Nature, her hair consists of 'snakes that terrify with fire' and lashes

ferociously around her forehead and body. She represents the force and vitality of the thoughts of the Father below the Supernals, and in a sense is a lesser form of Aion who is believed to perform a similar function above. Aion is also the force behind the sun, whereas Hecate is clearly identified with the moon.

In the Chaldean system links are provided between the initial Supernal triad and the subsequent emanations of the World Soul. These are called 'connectives', and the Supreme Father is therefore called the 'Connective of all Sources', meaning the originator of all ensuing emanations.

Each 'Sphere' has its own magical name, supplied by the Father, and these constitute his *thoughts*. The name, however, is not resident in the sphere but descends to it when invoked. Knowledge of such ineffable names was vital for the Theurgist if he was to 'bind' the god as part of his own mystical ascent.

This point emerges more clearly when we consider the manifested Cosmos in terms of the three 'World Circles' into which it was divided. The Chaldean Oracles labelled the outermost one, the Empyrean or Intelligible and assigned Aion as its 'ruler'. The next circle the Ethereal was that of the stars and planets, and was under the dominion of Apollo, the Sun. The inner 'world circle' was called Hyle, and enclosed the Moon and Earth, having Hecate as its 'ruler'.

Each 'ruler' had the function of providing purification and was therefore accorded great prominence in the Chaldean rites, Aion being 'the First Ruler of the Mysteries', and the source of Light illuminating the Mystic Sun.

Like the Greeks, the Neoplatonic theurgists found the Supernals rather remote from mankind. We find therefore that 'the principal function necessary for the accomplishment of the Chaldean mysteries is assigned to the sun and to its rays', for the Sun constitutes the symbolic 'high point' beneath the Supernal triad.

Nevertheless the force sustaining the Sun, derives as we have said from the loftier Aion, and it pours down through the 'connectives', 'which disseminate life, movement and intelligence throughout the Universe and preserve its harmonious existence'. The connectives are vital to the initiate as 'vehicles of theurgical ascension' for it is upon such solar rays that the soul will ascend after the invocation. The noetic substance, the 'body' of the Supernals, is fire, as in medieval alchemy, and it is said to be 'inhaled in mighty flames that descend from the Father, by Aion, who transmits it *to those who turn their "eye"* [144] *towards it*'.

Lewy writes: Union with the Light was 'the supreme goal of the Theurgists (and) . . . could only be attained through initiation into the sacramental mystery of immortality.[145] The rites of initiation symbolised the spatial stages of the soul's elevation, and were therefore 'expressions of spiritual experiences'.

Psellus says that the individual could not be 'elevated' unless the vehicle of the soul was 'strengthened'. Now the soul already contained a spark of the Cosmic Soul, bound through Eros, the Harmonizer, to portions of Intellect and Will, and descended into its present human framework from a much higher station. However, the descent of the soul through the intermediary zones between Godhead and Man had left the soul tainted by the influence of the stars and Hylic demons passed on the way.[146] The task of the Theurgist, in a very real sense, was to return his soul to its original, 'primitive' state.

As in the Graeco-Roman schools, this process involved the shamanistic separation of the soul from the body, and the ascension through archetypal visions confirmed as true, man's belief in immortality. 'The soul is saved for when (she) contemplates the blessed visions, she takes in exchange another

---

[144] The 'eye of the soul', a term coined by Plato.
[145] Hans Lewy: *Chaldean Oracles and Theurgy*, p. 178.
[146] In a similar fashion Porphyry regarded the tale of the war between the Athenians and the inhabitants of Atlantis as an allegory of the struggle between souls striving upwards and those drawn down into Hyle. Poseidon as god of the Sea, was also the personification of the senses, according to Numenius. Athens symbolised Reason and the victory of Athens showed the triumph of reason over passions and materialism.

life . . . and she no longer believes that she is a human mortal.'[147]

Ritual formulae, as we have noted, assisted in the mystical quest. The Chaldeans believed that the soul, in its pure state, understood very well the magical names, because both were of the nature of the Father. With the descent into matter, however, such knowledge was forgotten. The utterance of the 'names of power' not only produced the desired 'binding' effect but constituted a re-awakening—a return to the source. The solar rays bent down towards the initiate and lifted his soul towards the 'heart' (of the Sun).

Certain stages have been identified in the Chaldean rites of initiation:

I   *The Conjunction.* The Theurgist seeks the accompaniment of a god or daimen to grant him power for the accomplishment of the task. It is achieved by a rite involving an invocation with appropriate magical names. Psellus notes that Julian the Chaldean invoked 'all the gods' in conjunction, that is to say, an entire pantheon. Alternatively this could refer merely to the three Rulers: Aion, Apollo and Hecate. The timing of the operation was also important because the 'lords of the hour' were asked to look with favour upon the task at hand.

Psellus also says that an act of purification was made, consisting of a sacrifice of spices, plants or stones, mystically purified with fire. These were buried in a circle and on the following day lifted up out of the ground.

II *The Invocation* could now be made, and it was addressed to:
— the 'Masters of the Hylic substances' (the consecrated offerings previously buried in the ground).
— the Ruler of the Day
— the Lord of Time (Aion)

[147] Hans Lewy: *Chaldean Oracles and Theurgy*, p. 190. Note that the soul, as an aspect of Psyche, is represented as feminine.

— the Teacher of Sacrifice (Apollo, god of stones and herbs used in magic)
— the Daimon Lord of the Four (probably the four seasons of the year, symbolized by the Zodiac worn on the Chaldean vestments).[148]

The Theurgist meanwhile, having purified himself ritually, lay upon the ground, simulating bodily death, and covered his body, but not his head (from which his soul would emerge).

A companion daimon now stood between the initiate and Hades, ready to ward off the terrifying demons and phantoms from the bowels of the earth, who were ready to tempt the Theurgist 'away from the gifts of the gods and (lure him) towards matter'.

III *The Conjuration of the 'Binding Spirit'* was addressed through ineffable divine names to Apollo, symbol of the goal of elevation, and to Hecate. We have a fine description from Proclus and Psellus, of the archetypal vision of Hecate:

'Thou shalt either see a fire like a child, stretched over the vortex of the air, or a formless fire, from which a voice rushes forth, or an abundant light, rumbling spiralwise round the field. Thou mayest also see a horse flashing more brightly than light, or a boy sitting upon the back of a swift horse, a fiery (boy) or one covered over with gold or a naked one, or one shooting with a bow and standing on a horse.'[149] Hecate is preceded by fiery phantoms who become visible as forerunners in the 'binding spell'. When it is repeated she herself comes forth; in their midst. 'When thou dost behold the formless, most sacred fire flashing with quivering flames

---

[148] This is Lewy's suggestion. The absence of Hecate from this Invocation is surprising however. Possibly she is the Lord of the Four, in her capacity as Ruler of the Moon, and her identification also as the goddess of Nature, Intellect and the Earth.
[149] Proclus: *In Platonis Rempublicam commentar I.*

through the depths of the whole world, then hasten to the voice of the fire.'[150] (Hecate manifested fire, her actual appearance being sheathed in flame and not visible as a corporal shape.)

IV *Spiritual Rebirth.* The soul, having been conjured forth by the officiant of the ceremony, ascends on the solar rays, and is reborn into a new superhuman life. The Chaldeans held that the full splendour of this enterprise could only be experienced after death, but considered that the spiritual purity earned by the initials in this ceremony would at least ensure safe and direct passage to the heavenly realms in times to come. There would be no possibility of his becoming ensnared in the torture-regions of the afterworld. The initiate, in a sense, freed himself from the Judgement by so doing, but in both the Egyptian and the Platonic conceptions, the deceased really 'judges himself', automatically, as a matter of course.

Iamblichus writes that 'the theurgical ascent is a re-elevation and transition to a more excellent condition of being'.[151] He also stresses that purity is pragmatically necessary for otherwise the encountered visions would become 'turbulent and false' and no longer of use. Guthrie wrote much the same thing about the Orphic religion in Greece; stressing that the degree of purity affected the heights of heaven reached. For there *was* a higher heaven than Elysium. The aim of the Orphic was to 'become pure or clean. The uninitiated and immoral were thus unclean,'[152] he writes. Elysium was not the final home of the deified Orphic soul, for this place, in the strict usage of the term 'belonged properly to the *sublunar* order

---

[150] Psellus: *Commentaries.* Quoted in Lewy, p. 244.
[151] Iamblichus. *On the Mysteries* trans. Thomas Taylor. Stuart and Watkins, London, Ch. VII, p. 126.
[152] W. K. C. Guthrie: *Orpheus and Greek Religion.* Methuen, London, 1952, p. 164.

of things as much as Tartaros. Yet that the soul should go to Heaven seems to have been a familiar idea. . . . The word used is not usually Heaven but *aither*. *Aither* was the substance which filled the pure outer reaches of Heaven, beyond the impure atmosphere which surrounds the earth and extends as far as the moon. It was in this pure region that divinity dwelt, and the *aither* itself was supposed to be divine. In Euripides it appears now as the home of Zeus, now as Zeus himself. Those, then who believed the soul to be immortal and divine, were naturally inclined to suppose it to be made of an imprisoned spark of *aither*, which when set free would fly off to rejoin its like.'

Virgil *(Aeneid VI)* concurs in this idea—Elysium is the place of those who have had their final incarnation and those who will be reborn. Those who are totally pure 'go . . . to the stars, . . . leaving the regions of Elysium'.[153]

It is clear, however, in modification of the above, that the soul could only be freed from its 'tomb' if the Theurgist were pure, for without this condition the wrath of the deities would be incurred and Hecate would unleash her miscreant demons.

Given ritual purity, and words of power, the propitiant would be spiritually reborn in the vision of the mystical Light. A final word needs to be said here, though, and it is well said by Iamblichus. It concerns the emphasis in the Chaldean Oracles on causing the gods to descend. As Iamblichus says, *it is really we who are lifted up*. The power of the invocation 'does not draw down the impassive and pure Gods to that which is passive and impure; but on the contrary, it renders us, who have become passive through generation, pure and immutable.

'Neither do the invocations which implore the Gods to *incline* to us, conjoin the priests to them through passion; but procure for them the communion of an indissoluble connexion, through the *friendship which binds all things together*. Hence, it does

[153] W. K. C. Guthrie: *Orpheus and Greek Religion*, pp. 185–6.

not, as the name seems to imply, incline the intellect of the God to men; but according to the decision of truth, renders the will of man adapted to the participation of the Gods, (and) elevates it to them. . . .'[154]

[154] Iamblichus. *On the Mysteries*, Ch. XII, pp. 56–7.

CHAPTER FOUR

The Qabalah and the Tree of Life

We return finally to the Qabalah, a complex system of mysticism, which Western magic has employed extensively, and which in a sense represents a summation of earlier traditions. Although the *Zohar* (*circa* A.D. 1280), the central book of the Qabalah, was probably written by the Spaniard Moses de Leon, it has clear spiritual links with the earlier schools of Gnosticism and Neoplatonism. In all three, are present a series of emanations from the Godhead, the pre-existence of the soul and its descent into matter, and the emphasis on the sacred, ineffable names of God, the First Mystery. All three allude to the Father and Mother of creation, and in Gnosticism and the Qabalah we find a notable parallel between Sophia and Binah, the Supernal 'Wombs of Creation'. The Gnostic 'Pleroma' resembles the concept of the Qabalistic Tree of Life as the symbolic Body of God, and in all three systems we find the cyclic journey of the soul, through a succession of existences, towards union with *the source*.

In the Qabalah, all manifestations are said to have their origin in Ain Soph, the Infinite, the hidden God who 'has neither qualities nor attributes'. His subsequent emanations, however, reveal *aspects* of his divine nature, as portions of a mysterious Whole. Ain Soph, writes Scholem, 'manifests himself to the Kabbalist under ten different aspects, which in turn comprise an endless variety of shades and gradations'.[155] But the emanations in themselves constitute a Unity, the symbolic Body of God, so to speak. Ain Soph is the Life force of the Tree, Otz Chiim, the ten-fold symbol of emanations. But because man was created in the image of God, the world of the Sephiroth, and of God the Creator can also be visualized as the body of Adam Kadmon, the primordial man.

As with the Egyptians, the Universe is upheld by the utterance of the Holy Names, and the Sephiroth, or emanations are none other than 'the creative names which God called into the world, the names which He gave to Himself'.[156]

In the Zohar we read:

> 'In the Beginning, when the will of the King began to take effect, he engraved signed into the divine aura. A dark flame sprang forth from the innermost recess of the mystery of the infinite, Ain Soph, like a fog which forms out of the formless, enclosed in the ring of this aura, neither white nor black, neither red nor green, and of no colour whatever. But when this flame began to assume size and extension it produced radiant colours. For in the innermost centre of the flame a well sprang forth from which flames poured upon everything below, hidden in the mysterious secrets of Ain Soph. The well broke through, and yet did not entirely break through, the ethereal aura which surrounded it. It was entirely unrecognizable until under the impact of its break through a hidden Supernal point shone forth. Beyond this point nothing may be known or understood, and therefore it is called *Reshith*, that is "Beginning", the first word of creation.'

Scholem writes that the 'Primordial Point' was thought of by the majority of the Qabalists not as Kether, the Crown, but in the form of the Great Father Chokmah, Wisdom. His energy overpowered, and from the womb of Binah, the Supernal Mother, came forth all archetypal Forms. The seven subsequent emanations beneath this Triad constitute the seven days of Creation.

---

[155] Gersham G. Scholem: *Major Trends in Jewish Mysticism*. Schocken Books, New York, 1961, p. 209.
[156] Gersham G. Scholem: *Major Trends in Jewish Mysticism*. pp. 215-16.

Ginsburg echoes this view too: 'It is not the En-Soph, who created the world, but this Trinity,' that is to say, the Supernal triad. For 'the world was born from the union of the crowned King and Queen . . . who, emanated from the En Soph, produced the Universe in their own image'.[157]

The full sequence of emanations is as follows:

> KETHER—*The Crown* or Monad
>
> CHOKMAH—The Father, *Wisdom*
>
> BINAH—The Mother, *Understanding*
>
> CHESED—*Mercy*
>
> GEBURAH—*Severity*
>
> TIPHARETH—The Son, *Beauty* and *Harmony*
>
> NETZACH—*Victory*
>
> HOD—*Splendour*
>
> YESOD—The *Foundation*
>
> MALKUTH—The Daughter, *Kingdom*

The emanations align themselves into three Pillars, the outer two being the Pillars of *Mercy* (Male) headed by Chokmah, the Father and *Severity* (Female) headed by Binah the Mother. Beneath them lies the Garden of Eden, with its four rivers Chesed, Geburah, Netzach and Hod converging in Tiphareth, their Son, who resides as the central emanation on the Middle Pillar. A. E. Waite writes that perhaps this Pillar can be regarded as the Tree of Life itself,[158] for it resolves extremes, and reaches to the crown, Kether. The two other Pillars thus

---

[157] C. Ginsburg: *The Kabbalah*. Routledge and Kegan Paul/Macmillan. London, 1956. p. 102.
[158] A. E. Waite: *The Secret Doctrine in Israel*. O.M.T.B.C., Boston, 1914, p. 36.

become 'The Tree of Knowledge of Good and Evil'. The Gnostics and 'Chaldeans' saw the world as evil[159] because, as Matter, it was the grossest emanation, the furthest removed from the Godhead. In the Qabalah, Malkuth, the Kingdom (and the World), and the lowest upon the Tree, is a lesser form of the Great Mother, which may explain why her Pillar is called the Pillar of Severity (and Evil). It is clearly the dualism between Force and Form, the conflict of opposites expressed so well in the seminal Iranian cosmology, and which has to be resolved. Chesed and Geburah unite in the sixth, harmonizing Sephirah, Tiphareth.

Beneath these are formed Netzach, the personification of Nature and Love; Hod its opposition in rational Intellect; and their reconciler in Yesod, the Foundation of the Tree, and symbol of the fluid astral imagery, which changes like the Phases of the Moon ascribed to it. This triad of the Moon is thus a reflection of the preceding triad of the Sun, and when incorporated with the Earth, (Malkuth—the Kingdom) below, forms a fundamental trinity common to a large number of ancient pantheons.

We have alluded earlier to certain parallels between the great pantheons, and this has proved to be one of the most valuable aspects of the Tree of Life, for the deities of Egypt, Greece, Rome and the Neoplatonists can with some certainty be ascribed to certain Sephiroth upon the Tree.[160] As archetypes, they add an additional dimension to the Qabalistic structure, because unlike the Sephiroth, which are the Divine Names of one God, the hierarchical deities of the other systems tend to be represented as existing *in their own right*.

In the Egyptian god Nu, the Chaos of the Primordial Waters, we find a parallel for Ain Soph, and in Chokmah, Thoth, Kronos, Saturn and 'Mythes', we find Supernal Father archetypes who have an important generative function within their

---
[159] Specifically the world of Hyle, incorporating also the Moon but not the greater, deified planets.
[160] See also Appendix B.

respective pantheons. Binah, Isis, Rhea and the Chaldean 'Mother-Artisan' are the Mothers of the Gods, the Wombs of Forthcoming. Below these Idealized forms, which remain as 'constant factors' within the Cosmos, are located a new range of deities, headed once again by a paternal, energy-providing deity who is often considered to be the Demiurge and his female, receptive counterpart Ra and his wife Hathor, who is also his daughter, have this capacity. So, too, do Greek Zeus and his wives Hera and Demeter, brother Poseidon and Amphitrite, and their Roman counterparts, Jupiter, Juno, Neptune and Amphitrite.

Their offspring, or that of the Supernal triad symbolizes universally the goal of the mystical quest, for the neophyte seeks to become the child of the Gods, to be reawakened from his illusory mortal existence, into the realm of Spirit and Immortality. Correspondingly he identifies with the resurrected deity of Life and Harmony, ascribed to Tiphareth, and which takes the deified form of Osiris-Horus, Apollo, Dionysus or Christ. Below him in the Qabalah, are two emanations, Netzach and Hod which have important parallels in the Egyptian Hathor-Anubis, the Greek Aphrodite-Hermes, the Roman Venus-Mercury and in the 'Chaldean' Psyche-Hecate. Yesod heads this triad as the Foundation of the Tree, and significantly takes the important form of the Moon goddess, the partner of the Sun, and recipient of his Light. Bast, Hecate and Diana are archetypal parallels at this level. Beneath them are the personifications of Earth—Geb, Persephone and Proserpine, described in the Qabalah as the Virgin, or the Daughter of the Mighty Ones. And we are reminded that often the entry to higher (and lower) forms of consciousness is shamanistically represented as a cave in the earth, which leads upwards to Elysion or downwards to Hell.

Creation, in the Qabalah, unfolds through the utterance of the names of God, and these are the aspects of Deity assigned to each sphere.

However, the Qabalists, influenced perhaps by the elaborate

Iranian angelology, conceived of four 'divisions of being' within each Sephirah. The most refined is *Atziluth* which takes the God-name. However, the subsequent Worlds of 'degree' are: *Briah* governed by an Archangel, *Yetzirah* with the Angelic Host, and *Assiah* with its Mundane Chakras. Between Binah and Yesod, these take the form of the seven 'planets': Saturn; Jupiter; Mars; Sun; Venus; Mercury and the Moon, Kether being accorded the 'Primum Mobile', the 'First Swirlings', and Chokmah the totality of the Zodiac. In Malkuth, the Assiatic form of emanation within the Sephirah is represented by the Four Elements Air, Fire, Water and Earth taken as a whole.[161]

The Western magician whose aim it is to enter Tiphareth, follows the sequence of emanations, from Malkuth back towards their source. He encounters the archetypes as visions on a higher plane of consciousness. His goal is to assimilate them into his own being, by a process of identification *whereby he becomes the God*. In his rituals, and in his imagination, he utters the sacred Name of the God, called 'hekau' by the Egyptians, and he adopts the posture known as the God-Form.

In *Liber VI*, Aleister Crowley writes that the vibration of the 'hekau' should be made with the arms outstretched, and the God-name imagined as occupying the life-breath as it enters the nostrils. The name then descends through the body, from the lungs to the heart, solar plexus, navel, genitals and feet. At this very moment the magician advances his left foot in the ritual form of Horus the Enterer. The name courses through the body and is hurled forth orally in a forceful, resonant vibration. The left foot is now withdrawn and the magician adopts the form of Harpocrates, also an aspect of Horus: His right forefinger rests upon his lips characterizing Silence.

Such actions when coupled with strong visualization impress upon the magician the feeling that he has *become* the deity whose forms he has imitated in ritual. The process of gods ruling man is now reversed so that the magician commands the gods. The

---

[161] A table of the Divine Names ascribed to the Sephiroth in the Four Worlds appears in Appendix C.

microcosm has become the macrocosm. It is the *magician*, who now utters the sacred names which sustain the universe.

Scholem has alluded to the contemporary application of the Qabalah by the magicians Eliphas Levi and Aleister Crowley. In cosmological terms the rituals of the Sephirothic grades of the Golden Dawn, of which Crowley was a member, are a shamanistic transition through the Earth, past the Moon to the Sun. However, in the same way that the emanations in the Chaldean Oracles are linked by 'connectives', so too are the Sephiroth linked by Paths. In modern usage the system of the Tarot has been used extensively because the major Tarot trumps align exactly as symbolic representatives of the archetypal experiences upon the Paths between the Sephiroth.

Taking as our course the 'journey of the Middle Pillar' from Malkuth through Yesod to Tipareth, we come first to Tau, the entry through the 'Cumaean Gates' to the underworld of the subconscious. The Tarot card of this Path *'The World'*, shows a naked androgyne, fusion of male and female, dancing within a wreath of myrtle, or wheat-grain, sacred to Persephone. The dancer holds spiral wands to symbolise the life-force and indicate that the journey into the domain of death can bring forth new life. In the corners of the card are portrayed the four symbols of resurrection, the Kerubic animals of the Tetragrammaton J H V H—Man, Lion, Eagle and Ox.

From Yesod to Tiphareth the magician travels upon Samekh, symbolised by the Tarot card *'Temperance'*, and called the Path of the Archer, Sagittarius. An angel is shown pouring the waters of Life from his right hand and bearing a torch in his left. This may be Raphael, but it could also be Iris the goddess of the rainbow—for the 'bow of promise' shines in the sky beyond.

The angel stands between a fiery lion, and an eagle, 'tempering' or 'conjoining' the creatures who are traditionally lords of earth and air. Mythologically their combination connotes the griffin, sacred to Sun, whose Sphere the Path of Samekh approaches. Paul Case identifies the angel as the Holy Guardian

Angel, 'the real I am, or Ego of the entire human race, having its seat in Tiphareth. . . .' He adds: 'The practical import of the picture is this: We do nothing of ourselves. The Holy Guardian Angel makes all the tests and trials which lead us along the path of attainment' . . . and upon his robe is written the name: 'That which was, and is, and shall be.'[162]

In the West the aspirant of High Magic as presented in the Hermetic Order of the Golden Dawn undergoes the grades of all the Sephiroth leading to Tiphareth. We have presented this sequence in a more fundamental form, as the journey upon the Middle Pillar, because it is upon this equilibrating Path that the cosmological significance of the transformation of consciousness can best be seen. Magic, like the shamanistic journey and the Egyptian passage through the Tuat, is *an entry into the Night-time of the Unconscious and a Coming-Forth by Day*. Accordingly, the following chapter is written only with the view of expressing the symbolism of the 'rebirth of the soul'.

[162] Paul F. Case: *The Tarot*. Macoy Publishing Company. New York, 1947, p. 152.

CHAPTER FIVE

Neophyte, Zelator, Theoricus, Adept

On the dais of the East, quarter of the rising sun, sit three Chiefs, representing Thoth, Isis and Nephthys, gods who assisted in the Osirian Resurrection. The Hierophant, Osiris himself, the god who is reborn, is also enthroned in their midst upon the mystical path Samekh, which leads to Harmony.

In the West is Hiereus representing Horus the Avenger, and in the North and South, Stolistes and Dadouchos, bearers of Water and Fire. In the South-West, Kerux and the Sentinel, forms of Anubis, guard the Sacred Hall to keep away intruders. Hegemon, personifying the goddess of truth, Maat, presides over the weighing of the scales of truth between the black and white Pillars near the centre. Here also is the altar of the Elements, showing its white upper face, symbol of light coming forth from darkness.

The Hierophant says:

'My station is on the Throne of the East in the place where the Sun rises and I am the Master of the Hall, governing it according to the Laws of the Order, as He whose Image I am, is the Master of all who work for the Hidden Knowledge. My robe is red because of Uncreated Fire and Created Fire and I hold the Banner of the Morning Light which is the Banner of the East. I am called Power and Mercy and Light and Abundance, and I am the Expounder of the Mysteries.'

The Hall is purified with Water and with Fire, and Kerux opens the 'Hall of the Neophytes' in the North East, facing West, and declaring:

'In the Name of the Lord of the Universe, who works in Silence and whom naught but Silence can express, I declare that the Sun has arisen and the Shadows flee away. . . .'

Robed and hooded so that he cannot see, the Neophyte ('child of the Earth') enters and is purified symbolically with Water and with Fire. He is questioned as to his purpose of entry and presents himself like Ani in the Hall of Maati, hopeful of rebirth:

'My Soul Wanders in Darkness and seeks the Light of the Hidden Knowledge. . . .' He pledges secrecy, undergoes ritual oaths and passes to the Northern quarter—home of Forgetfulness and Darkness.

He seeks to come forth from the Darkness, as Light from the Abyss.

After ritual purification the Neophyte now enters the gates of the West and of the East, headed by Kerux, and protected by the magical words of entry, the hekau, or ineffable formulae of power uttered by Hegemon, goddess of truth.

The Hierophant instructs that they pass onwards to the Cubical Altar of the Universe, where the Hierophant, standing to the East of the Altar and between the Mystical Pillars pronounces:

> 'I come in the Power of Light
> I come in the Light of Wisdom
> I come in the Mercy of the Light
> The Light hath Healing in its Wings'

The invocation to the Lord of the Universe is made, and the light of inspiration is sought upon the Neophyte. The Neophyte in imitation is brought between the Pillars and is taught the sign of the Enterer and the sign of Silence, both ascribed to Horus (the latter in his form as Harpocrates). Further purifications of Fire and Water are made and the Mystic Circumambulation of Light, the ritually enacted cyclic passage of the Sun through the Tuat, takes place. Circumambulation is reversed as an expression of fading Light, and the ceremonial comes to a close.

We have encountered the Hall of the Neophyte previously as the Hall of Maati in the Osirian *Books of the Dead*. In this ritual the four Sephiroth below Tiphareth (=the Sun, Osiris, resurrection) are represented as Netzach (Fire) in the South; Malkuth (Earth) in the West; Hod (Water) in the North and Yesod the Place of the Evil Triad.

Near the altar which bears the colours of Earth except for its numinous upper face, are the two Pillars of Mercy and Severity from the Tree of Life. The Hierophant (Osiris) stands as reconciler between them symbolising the Middle Way, the mystical path of ascent. We note that the Neophyte who later stands in his place is bound by a triple bond of rope symbolizing the funerary swathings of the god who is reborn.

Beyond the Hierophant in the region of the Veil Paroketh resides Hathor wearing the Disc of the Sun. She represents one of a number of *Invisible Stations*, mighty 'unconscious forces' which preside as unrepresented but inspirational forms over the ritual. In similar fashion we find the Kerubim: Man—Lion—Eagle—Ox, at the four Cardinal Points beyond the Hierophant, Dadouchos, Hiereus and Stolistes. Between these, the Lords of the Elements, the four Canopic gods, children of Horus. And in Yesod we find the Evil One, Set—Apophis—Typhon, the antagonist of Osiris and embodiment of chaos and destruction, who is overcome.

Zelator

An earth tablet and cup, the receptive Maiden, are placed in the North. Hiereus and Hegemon flank the altar and in the West stand Stolistes, Kerux and Dadouchos. The Hierophant resides at the entrance to the 32nd Path.

The Temple is purified with Water and Fire and an adoration

of Adonai ha Aretz, Lord of the Earth, is made by the Hierophant. Man becomes *Master of the Elements*:

And the Elohim said: 'Let us make Adam in our Image, after our likeness and let him have dominion over the fish of the sea and over the fowl of the air and over the cattle and over all the earth. . . .'

In the Name of Uriel, the Great Archangel of Earth, and by the sign of the Head of the Ox—Spirits of Earth, adore Adonai!

> In the names of God: EMOR DIAL HECTEGA
> In the name of the Great King of the North: IC ZOD HE CHAL
> In the name of: ADONAI HA ARETZ

The Neophyte holding the Fylfot Cross, symbol of the Sun, Elements and Zodiac states his quest of knowledge. Having demonstrated the ritual signs of his grade he is led to the West and is positioned between the Pillars of Extremity, facing towards the East, quarter of the mystical Dawn. He casts forth the Salt of the Earth, and is purified by Fire and Water. The Hierophant instructs him in the Mysteries of his grade:

> 'And Tetragrammaton Elohim planted a Garden Eastward in Eden, and out of the ground made Jehovah Elohim to grow every tree that is pleasant to the sight and good for food; the Tree of Life also, in the midst of the Garden, and the Tree of Knowledge of Good and of Evil. This is the Tree that has two Paths, and it is the Tenth Sephira Malkuth, and it has about it Seven Columns, and the Four Splendours whirl around it as in the Vision of the Mercabah of Ezekiel; and from Gedulah it derives an influx of Mercy, and from Geburah an influx of Severity, and the Tree of the Knowledge of Good and of Evil shall it be until it is united with the Supernals in Daath.
>
> 'But the Good which is under it is called the Archangel Metatron and the Evil is called the Archangel Samael, and between them lies the straight and narrow way where the Archangel Sandalphan keeps watch. The Souls and the Angels are above its branches, and the Qlippoth or Demons dwell under its roots.'

The Neophyte now passes to the region of Samael where he is instructed by the Prince of Darkness, and to the region of Metatron where he learns of the Ineffable Light of the Creator god. Passing along the way of mediation between them he encounters Sandalphon, 'reconciler for Earth', who 'prepares the way to the Celestial Light'.

Emerging from Malkuth are three Paths: Tau, Qoph and Shin, forming 'Qesheth' the Bow of Promise.

The Neophyte is led out and the Temple transforms to represent the Holy Court of the Tabernacle, the place of Burnt Sacrifice. Having returned the Neophyte is purified with Fire and Water and passes to the entrance between the Pillars where he demonstrates the ritual signs of the Neophyte and the Zelator of Malkuth. The Neophyte is told the secrets of the Bread of Life, the Rose of Creation, the Lamp of the Sun and the Zodiacal Signs. He learns the symbolic basis of the Jewish alphabet of manifestation and the connotations of the altar of the Elements. Thus he is given the grade of the Sephirah Malkuth, the 'Gate of the Daughter of the Mighty Ones' and entrance to the mystical Garden of Eden.

Theoricus

The temple remains as before. Kerux resides in the North, Hegemon in the South, Hiereus in the West, and the Hierophant in the East.
An adoration is made to the King of Air, Shaddai El Chai:

"'And the Elohim said: 'Let us make Adam in Our Image after our likeness, and let them have dominion over the Fowl of the Air.

> In the Names YOD HE VAU HE and
> SHADDAI EL CHAI
> In the name of the Great Archangel RAPHAEL
> In the names of ORO IBAH AOZPI
> and BATAIVAH, Spirits of Air. . . .'"

Theoricus represents the first step beyond Matter towards the Spiritual. The Zelator enters, and provides the signs of his ritual grade. Embodying the profound paradox of death which leads to rebirth, he takes as his guide the Egyptian Anubis, the master embalmer whose knowledge assisted Osiris in the Resurrection: 'I am the *synthesis* of the Elemental Forces. I am also the symbol of Man. I am Life and I am Death. I am the Child of the Night of Time.' Kerux and Zelator approach the Gate of the East, which opens on the utterance of the names of Nu, the Air, and Hormaku, the Lord of the Eastern Sun.

Zelator is now purified by the four-fold symbols of the Resurrection—MAN (Osiris) LION (Mau) EAGLE (Heka) and OX (Satem)—and comes between the Pillars.

The Hierophant instructs him concerning the twenty-two sacred letters upon the Cubical Cross, which make up the Vault of Heaven. Zelator also learns of the symbolism of the Maiden of the Twenty-First Tarot Key, the goddess Persephone whom we have alluded to before as Queen of the Underworld and who dwells in the region between Earth and Moon. He is taught the sacred seventy-two fold Name of God, and the names of the Elemental Orders—Sylphs (Air); Salamanders (Fire); Undines (Water) and Gnomes (Earth) which are rendered visible in the astral vision.

Zelator is led out, and returns to the Temple which now represents the Path Tau. Before him on the altar are the symbols of the Tree of Life—the twenty-two letters and the ten Sephirah making the thirty-two fold Path of Wisdom, and the Cross within the triangle (representing the four rivers of Eden within Netzach Hod and Yesod, and the conjunction of Male Female, Adam and Eve).

Zelator receives the symbol of the Ruach and the grade of Theoricus and an adoration is made to SHADDAI EL CHAI; which parellels the Egyptian *Opening of the Mouth*, the infusion of Life into that which was dead: . . . 'O Imperishable Breath of Life! O Creative Sigh,! O Mouth which breathest forth and withdrawest the life of all beings, in the flux and reflux of

Thine Eternal Word, which is the Divine Ocean of Movement and of Truth!'

Adept

We approach now towards the Inner Sanctum, the Ruby Rose and the Cross of Gold, profound symbols of Man's rebirth.

In the *Ritual of the Portal of the Vault of the Adepti*—Philosophus, (so called because in normal Golden Dawn sequence he has also earned the grades of Hod and Netzach) stands in the Primordial Darkness, 'The Realm of Chaos and of Ancient Night.' The Dragon of the Qlippoth rages triumphant in the deep until Thoth utters the Word of Creation which brings forth Light. Philosophus prepares to receive the mysteries of the same transformation, from Duality to Unity, and relives the visions through which he has already passed.

In the *Rite of the Pentagram and the Fire Paths* he is accorded mastery over the Paths of Light which come forth from the dark: Mem; Ayin; Samekh; Nun; and Kaph symbolising the Pentagram of Microscopic Man.

Philosophus is reminded of Qesheth, the Bow of Promise, and the Arrow 'Samekh, soaring upward to cleave open the Veil unto the Sun in Tiphareth'. Its sender, Sagittarius the Archer, has within his scope, the lofty path of Kaph, which encroaches upon Jupiter, Lord and Demiurge of the manifested Cosmos:

'There is vision of the fire-flashing courser of Light, or also a child borne aloft upon the shoulders of the Celestial Steed, fiery or clothed with gold, or naked and shooting from the bow, shafts of light, and standing on the shoulders of a horse. But if thy meditation prolongeth itself thou shalt unite all these symbols in the form of a Lion, reconciler in Teth, of Mercy and Severity beneath whose centre hangs the glorious Sun of Tiphareth.'

Philosophus must now sacrifice his lower self upon the Cross of the Four Elements, in the name of Paroketh, the veil whose name incorporates Peh (Water); Resh (Air); Kaph (Fire) and Tau (Earth).

'It is the Word of the Veil, the Veil of the Tabernacle, of the Temple, before the Holy of Holies, the Veil which was rent asunder. It is the Veil of the Four Elements of the Body of Man which was offered upon the Cross for the Service of Man.... This is the sign of the rending of the Veil....'

Philosophus has now become the Lord of the Paths of the Portal of the Vault of the Adepti.

In the *Ceremony of the Grade of Adeptus Minor* (Tiphareth) the candidate himself is *Hodos Chamelionis*, Lord of the Lights upon the Path of the Chameleon. He undergoes a symbolic burial and emergence in the Tomb of the Adepti identifying with Christian Rosenkreutz, the Rose and Cross of the Immortal Christ, and the risen Osiris. The tomb has seven sides representing the seven lower Sephiroth beneath the Supernal triad and the Seven 'Days' of Creation. It is situated symbolically *in the centre of the Earth* just as Tiphareth resides *in the centre of the Tree of Life*. The spiritual rebirth occurs after 'one hundred and twenty years' which are the ten Sephiroth multiplied by the twelve signs of the Zodiac, and it follows ritually the form of the myth of Osiris whereby the body of the slain King of Egypt is magically revitalised. The five earlier rites, and death upon the Elemental Cross, have prepared the candidate for his entry into the Tomb of the Sacred Mountain.

Philosophus lies clothed with the symbols of the embalmed Osiris: the symbol of the Rosy Cross also rests upon his breast.

'Eternal One ... let the influence of thy Divine Ones descend upon his head, and teach him the value of self-sacrifice so that he shrink not in the hour of trial, but that thus his name may be written on high and that his Genius may stand in the presence of the Holy Ones, in that hour when the Son of Man is invoked before the Lord of Spirits and His Name in the presence of the Ancient of Days. It is written: "If any man will come after Me, let him take up his cross, and deny himself, and follow Me".'

Philosophus extends his arms so that his body forms a cross, the ritual expression of rebirth:

'Buried with that Light in a mystical death, rising again in a mystical resurrection . . . Quit then this Tomb, O Aspirant, (whose arms have been earlier) crossed upon thy breast, bearing in thy right hand the Crook of Mercy, and in thy left the Scourge of Severity, the emblems of those Eternal Forces betwixt which the equilibrium of the universe dependeth; those forces *whose reconciliation is the Key of Life*, whose separation is evil and death. . . .'

The Aspirant, filled with light, now comes forth as Christ—Osiris, by day.

'And being turned, I saw Seven Golden Lightbearers, and in the midst of the Lightbearers, One like unto the Ben Adam, clothed with a garment down to the feet, and girt with a Golden Girdle. His head and his hair were white as snow and His eyes as flaming fire; His feet like unto fine brass, as if they burned in a furnace. And His voice as the sound of many waters. And He had in His right hand Seven Stars, and out of His mouth went the Sword of Flame, and his countenance was as the Sun in His Strength.

'I am the First and I am the Last. I am He that liveth and was dead, and behold! I am alive for evermore, and hold the Keys of Death and of Hell. . . . I am the purified. I have passed through the Gates of Darkness into Light. . . .

'I am the Sun in his rising. I have passed through the hour of cloud and of night.

'I am Amoun, the Concealed One, the Opener of the Day. I am Osiris Onnophris, the Justified One.

'I am the Lord of Life triumphant over Death.

'*There is not part of me which is not of the Gods.*'

Appendix A: ARCHETYPAL CORRESPONDENCES

EGYPTIAN	GREEK	ROMAN	'CHALDEAN'	('RULERS')	QABALAH
PTAH (Memphis) ATUM-RA (Heliopolis) AMON (Thebes)	KRONOS	SATURN	ALL-FATHER, 'MYTHES'		KETHER (Eheieh)
THOTH				AION (Persian Zurvan, Gnostic Abraxas, Greek Kronos)	CHOKMAH (Jehovah) *FATHER*
ISIS	RHEA	RHEA	MOTHER-POWER, 'ARTISAN'		BINAH (Jehovah Elohim) *MOTHER*
RA	ZEUS (Hera, Demeter) POSEIDON (Amphitrite) ARES	JUPITER (Juno) NEPTUNE (Amphitrite) MARS	SON-'IDEAS'		CHESED (El) *DEMIURGE*
HORUS (Warrior), RA, OSIRIS-HORUS	HELIOS-APOLLO, DIONYSUS	APOLLO		APOLLO	GEBURAH (Elohim Gebor) TIPHARETH (Jehovah Aloah Va Daath) NETZACH (Jehovah Tzabaoth) *SON*
HATHOR	APHRODITE	VENUS			
ANUBIS BAST	HERMES HECATE, ARTEMIS	MERCURY DIANA	PSYCHE-HECATE, 'WORLD SOUL'	HECATE	HOD (Elohim Tzabaoth) YESOD (Shaddai El Chai)
GEB	PERSEPHONE	PROSERPINE			MALKUTH (Adonai Ha-Aretz) *DAUGHTER*

145

Appendix B: THE DIVINE NAMES ATTRIBUTED TO THE SEPHIROTH

SEPHIRAH	DIVINE NAME (Atziluth)	ARCHANGELIC NAME (Briah)	CHOIR OF ANGELS (Yetsirah)	MUNDANE CHAKRAS (Assiah)
1. Kether	Eheieh	Metatron	Chayoth ha-Qadesh	Primum Mobile, First Swirlings
2. Chokmah	Jehovah	Raziel	Auphanim	Mazloth, the Zodiac
3. Binah	Jehovah Elohim	Tzaphqiel	Aralim	Saturn
4. Chesed	El	Tzadquiel	Chashmalim	Jupiter
5. Geburah	Elohim Gebor	Kamael	Seraphim	Mars
6. Tiphareth	Jehovah Aloah Va Daath	Raphael	Melekim	The Sun
7. Netzach	Jehovah Tzabaoth	Haniel	Elohim	Venus
8. Hod	Elohim Tzabaoth	Michael	Beni Elohim	Mercury
9. Yesod	Shaddai El Chai	Gabriel	Kerubim	The Moon
10. Malkuth	Adonai ha-Aretz	Sandalphon	Ashim	The Four Elements

BIBLIOGRAPHY

ANGUS, SAMUEL: *The Mystery Religions and Christianity.* University Books, New York, 1966.
BALIKCI, ASEN: 'Shamanistic Behavior among the Netsilik Eskimos' in *Magic, Witchcraft and Curing.* Ed. John Middleton, Natural History Press, New York, 1967.
BARDON, FRANZ: *The Practice of Magical Evocation.* Rudolf Pravica, Graz-Puntigam, Austria, 1967.
BEATTIE, JOHN: 'Divination in Bunyoro, Uganda' in *Magic, Witchcraft and Curing.* Ed. John Middleton, Natural History Press, New York, 1967.
BELOFF, JOHN: *The Existence of Mind.* MacGibbon and Kee, London, 1962.
BOLTON, J. D. P.: *Aristeas of Proconnesus.* Clarendon Press, Oxford, 1962.
BORGES, JORGE LUIS: *The Book of Imaginary Beings.* Discus-Avon Books, New York, 1969.
BUDGE, E. A. WALLIS: *Amulets and Talismans.* University Books, New York, 1961.
— *The Bandlet of Righteousness.* Luzac, London, 1929.
— *The Egyptian Book of the Dead.* Routledge & Kegan Paul, London. Second edition, eighth impression, 1960.
— *The Egyptian Heaven and Hell.* Martin Hopkinson, London, 1925.
BULFINCH, THOMAS: *Mythology.* The Modern Library, New York, n.d.
BUTLER, W. E.: *The Magician, His Training and Work.* Aquarian, London, 1959.
CARPENTER, E.: *The Act of Creation.* Allen & Unwin, London, 1907.
CASE, PAUL F.: *The Tarot.* Macoy Publishing Company, New York, 1947.
CASTANEDA, C.: *A Separate Reality.* The Bodley Head, London, 1971.
CLARK, R. T. RUNDLE: *Myth and Symbol in Ancient Egypt.* Thames & Hudson, London, 1959.
CORNFORD, F. M.: *Plato's Republic.* Clarendon Press, Oxford, 1941.
CROOKALL, R.: *The Jung-Jaffe View of Out-of-the-Body Experiences.* W.F.P., Plymouth, 1970.

CROWLEY, ALEISTER: *Book Four*. Wieland & Co., London, c. 1911–12.
— *Magick in Theory and Practice*. Castle Books, New York, n.d.
CUMONT, F.: *The Mysteries of Mithra*. Dover Publications, New York, 1956.
DODDS, E. R.: *The Greeks and the Irrational*. University of California, Berkeley, 1951.
DRURY, N. AND SKINNER, S.: *The Search for Abraxas*. Neville Spearman, London, 1973.
ELIADE, M.: *Shamanism: Archaic Techniques of Ecstasy*. Routledge & Kegan Paul, London, 1964.
EVANS-WENTZ, W. Y.: *The Tibetan Book of the Dead*. Oxford University Press, New York, 1960.
FARR, F. (Soror S.S.D.D.): *Collectanea Hermetica Vol. VIII (Egyptian Magic)*. Theosophical Publishing Society, London, 1896.
FORTUNE, D.: *The Mystical Qabalah*. Benn, London, 1966.
GEERTZ, C.: 'Religion as a Cultural System' in *A.S.A.5*. Tavistock, London, 1966.
GINSBURG, C.: *The Kabbalah*. Routledge & Kegan Paul/Macmillan, London, 1956.
GREEN, CELIA: *Out-of-the-Body Experiences*. Institute of Psychophysical Research, Oxford, 1968.
GUTHRIE, W. K. C.: *Orpheus and Greek Religion*. Methuen, London, 1952.
IAMBLICHUS: *On the Mysteries*. Stuart & Watkins, London. Third edition, 1968.
IONS, VERONICA: *Egyptian Mythology*. Paul Hamlyn, Middlesex, 1968.
JACOBI, JOLANDE: *The Psychology of C. G. Jung*. Routledge & Kegan Paul, London, 1968.
JUNG, C. G. AND KERENYI, K.: *Essays on a Science of Mythology*. Harper & Row, New York, 1963.
JUNG, C. G.: *Man and His Symbols*. Dell, New York, 1968.
— *Two Essays on Analytical Psychology*. Routledge & Kegan Paul, London, 1953.
KERENYI, C.: *Eleusis*. Routledge & Kegan Paul, London, 1967.
KINGSLAND, W.: *The Gnosis or Ancient Wisdom in the Christian Scriptures*. George Allen & Unwin, London, 1937.
KNIGHT, GARETH: *A Practical Guide to Qabalistic Symbolism*. Vols. I and II. Helios, Cheltenham, 1965.
KNIGHT, W. F. JACKSON: *Elysion*. Rider & Co., London, 1970.
— *Vergil, Epic and Anthropology*. George Allen & Unwin, London, 1967.
LEARY, TIMOTHY et al.: *The Psychedelic Experience*. University Books, New York, 1964.

LEVI, ELIPHAS: *The Key of the Mysteries*. Rider & Co., London, 1959.
LEWIS, I. M.: *Ecstatic Religion*. Penguin Books, Harmondsworth, 1971.
LEWY, HANS: *Chaldean Oracles and Theurgy*. De L'Institut Francais D'Archeologie Orientale, Cairo, 1956.
MAETERLINCK, M.: *The Great Secret*. University Books, New York, 1969.
MALINOWSKI, B.: *Magic, Science and Religion*. Beacon Press, Boston, 1948.
MARTINO, ERNEST DE: *Magic, Primitive and Modern*. Bay Books, Sydney, 1972.
METZNER, R.: *Maps of Consciousness*. Macmillan, New York, 1971.
ROHDE, E.: *Psyche*. Kegan Paul, Trench, Trubner, London, 1925.
RUSSELL, GEORGE (A. E.): *The Candle of Vision*. Macmillan, London, 1920.
SAINT-GERMAIN, COMTE DE: *The Most Holy Trinosophia*. Philosophers' Press, Los Angeles, 1949.
SALE, GEORGE (trans.): *The Koran*. William Tegg, London, n.d.
SCHOLEM, G. G.: *Major Trends in Jewish Mysticism*. Schocken Books, New York, 1961.
SPIRO, MELFORD E.: 'Religion, Problems of Definition and Explanation' in *A.S.A.5*. Tavistock, London, 1966.
WAITE, A. E.: *The Secret Doctrine in Israel*. O.M.T.B.C., Boston, 1914.
WALKER, K.: *Diagnosis of Man*. Pelican Books, Harmondsworth, 1962.
ZIMMER, H.: *Myths and Symbols in Indian Art and Civilization*. Harper & Row, 1962.

INDEX

Abraham, 44
Abraxas, 40
Adam, 42n, 140
Aeneas, 107, 111
Aeon, 40, 53, 54, 55, 56, 57, 70
Ahura-Mazda, 39
Ain Soph, 21, 66, 127, 128, 129, 130
Aion, 40, 116, 117, 120, 121, 122
Akawaio Carib, 33
Alchemy, 29
Alexander, 58
Allah, 41, 42, 43
Alpert, R., 83
Amenhotep, 45
Am Tuat, 84, 85, 87, 92n, 98, 99, 100
Angus, S., 48
Anubis, 87, 88, 94, 131, 135, 140
Aphrodite, 34, 131
Apollo, 25, 107, 113, 114, 115, 117, 118, 120, 122, 125, 131
Archetypes, 24, 25, 26, 27, 28, 33, 35, 64, 68, 81, 82, 84, 92, 121, 123, 128, 130, 132, 133
Aidoneus, (Hades), 26
Aristeas of Proconnesus, 83, 103, 104, 112, 113–115
Aristotle, 111
Artemis, 118
Asoka, 49
Assiah, 64, 66, 68
Atlantis, 121n
Atziluth, 64, 66, 68, 132
Aurelius, Marcus, 117
Avatar, 38

Balikci, A., 19n
Bardon, F., 69, 75
Bardo Thodol, 83, 85
Basilides, 40, 52,
Beattie, J., 20n
Bhagavad-Gita, 39
Binah, 27, 28, 63, 64, 74, 76, 127, 128, 129, 131, 132

Boas, F., 22
Body of Light, 71, 77
Book of Gates, 84, 85, 87, 92, 98, 99, 100
Borges, J. L., 115
Brandon, S. G. F., 40, 84, 104
Briah, 64, 66, 132
Bruce Codex, 54, 55
Buber, M., 36
Buddha, 49
Buddha-Heruka, 20
Buddhism, 20, 38n, 49, 50, 145
Bucke, R. M., 60, 62
Budge, Sir E. A. W., 40, 67, 84n, 86n, 100, 102n
Buryat, 33

Carpenter, E., 61
Case, P. F., 133, 134n
Castaneda, C., 33, 34n, 112n
Castor, 105
Centre of the World, 33
Cewa (Central Africa), 18
Chakras, 29, 65
Chaldean Oracles, 82, 116–126, 133
Chesed, 64, 76, 129, 130
Chokmah, 27, 28, 63, 64, 74, 75, 128, 129, 130
Christ, Jesus, 38n, 39, 42n, 44, 49, 50, 51, 52, 53, 54, 55, 56, 57, 58, 64n, 70, 81, 115, 131, 142, 143
Christianity, 38n, 41, 48, 51, 116
Clark, R., 84
Clement of Alexandria, 51
Collyridians, 41
Cornford, F., 108
Cranston, S. L., 51
Crookall, R., 30n, 111
Crowley, A., 63, 71, 72, 74, 76, 78, 132, 133

Daath, 77, 138
Dali, S., 65
Damascius, 119

Demeter, 26, 27, 34, 83, 105, 106, 131
Demiurge, 53, 119, 131, 141
Devi, S., 151
Diana, 107
Diaspora, 47
Dickinson, G. Lowes, 147
Dionysius the Areopagite, 25
Dionysus, 83, 106, 107, 110, 131
Dodds, E. R., 104, 107
Dreams, 23–24, 25
Dreamtime, The, 17, 82
Drury, N., 82n
Ducasse, C. J., 148–150

Ebionites, 52
Egyptian Book of the Dead, 67, 70, 100, 114, 137
Eleusis, 13, 26, 29, 34, 83, 105, 106
Eliade, M., 31, 33n
Elysian Fields, 85, 94, 98, 99, 100
Elysium, 124, 125
Er, Myth of, 108–111
Ernst, M., 65
Eros, 121
Evans-Pritchard, E. E., 15
Evans-Wentz, W. Y., 20n, 50n
Eve, 42n, 140
Existentialism, 35–37

Fortune, D., 71, 72n
Frazer, Sir J., 18
Freud, S., 15, 17, 18, 22, 23, 65

Garden of Eden, 129, 138, 139, 140
Geburah, 74, 76, 129, 130, 138
Gedulah, 74, 76, 138
Geertz, C., 15, 16, 17
Gilgamish, 104
Ginsburg, C., 129
Gnostics, 21, 25, 40, 51, 52, 53, 54, 55, 58, 62, 70, 116, 127, 130
Golden Dawn, Hermetic Order of, 14, 63, 75, 116, 133, 134, 141, 149
Graves, R., 147
Green, C., 15, 30, 31, 32n, 111, 147
Griffins (Gryphons), 113, 114, 115
Guthrie, W. K. C., 124, 125n

Hades, 26, 104, 106
Hathor, 88, 131, 137
Head, J., 51

Hecate, 26, 27, 34, 117, 118, 119, 120, 122, 123, 124, 125, 131
Hekau, 86, 101, 132, 136
Helios, 25, 26, 27, 118
Heracles, 28
Hermes, 26, 34, 118, 131
High Magic, 26, 38, 62, 83, 134
Hinduism, 38n, 145
Hod, 34, 64, 75, 129, 130, 131, 137, 140, 141
Hofmann, A., 106
Holy Guardian Angel, 68, 133, 134
Homer, 103
Horus, 85n, 89, 90, 91, 93, 94, 95, 96, 97, 101, 131, 132, 135, 136, 137
Huxley, Sir J., 146
Hyle, 55, 120, 121, 122, 130n

Iamblichus, 116, 119, 124, 125, 126n
Iglulik Eskimos, 31
Institute of Psychophysical Research, 31, 32n
Isis, 84–85n, 87, 88, 89, 101, 131
Islam, 43, 59

Jacobi, J., 28
Jaffe, A., 30
James, W., 38, 151
Judaism, 48, 52
Julian the Chaldean, 116, 117, 122
Julian the Theurgist, 116, 117
Jung, C. G., 15, 22, 23, 24, 25, 26, 27n, 28, 29, 30, 67, 68n

Kalahari, 33
Kerenyi, K., 26, 27n, 106, 107
Kether, 21, 29, 63, 64, 74, 75, 77, 128, 129, 132
Kierkegaard, S., 36
Kingsland, W., 52, 53n
Knight, W. F., Jackson, 104, 105n
Ko Hung, 29
Koran, 42n, 43
Kronos, 40, 130

Labisse, F., 65
Lamplugh, A. A. F., 51
Leary, T., 83
Lefefa Sedek, 57, 58, 70
Leon, Moses de, 127
Levi, E., 69, 133
Levi-Strauss, C., 24n, 81

151

Levy-Bruhl, L., 22
Lewy, H., 116, 118n, 119, 121, 123n

Maat, 70, 89, 94, 99, 135, 136, 137
Maeterlinck, M., 59
Magritte, R., 65
Malinowski, B., 16
Malkuth, 27, 65, 66, 74, 77, 130, 132, 133, 137, 138, 139
Marcel, G., 36
Marwick, M. G., 18
Mary, The Virgin, 41, 58, 70
Mathers, S. L., 71
Matus, Don Juan, 33, 35, 112n, 149
Maximus of Tyre, 112, 113, 114
McTaggart, J. E., 145, 146, 147, 150
Mead, G. R. S., 52, 53
Mercury, 118, 131
Metzner, R., 83
Middle Pillar, 29, 75n, 129, 133
Middleton, J., 15
Mishnah, 47
Mithra, 40, 116
Mohammed, 39, 41, 42, 43
Moses, 39, 41, 42, 43
Mounier, E., 36

Nephesch, 64, 65
Nephythys, 87, 135
Nerval, G. de, 13
Neschamah, 64
Neoplatonists, 116, 117, 118, 119
Netsilik Eskimos, 19
Netzach, 34, 76, 129, 130, 131, 137, 140, 141
Nu, 91, 95, 97, 98, 101, 130, 140
Nyoro tribe, 19

Ohrmazd, 25, 39
Olympus, 103, 105
Ophites, 52
Orpheus, 83, 105, 107, 110, 117, 118, 124
Osiris, 28, 67, 70, 73, 84, 85, 86, 87, 88, 89, 90, 91, 92, 94, 95, 96, 97, 98, 99, 100, 101, 115, 131, 135, 137, 140, 142, 143
Otz Chiim, 63, 128
Out-of-the-Body Experiences, 15, 30, 31, 32n, 71, 111, 114, 148
Ovid, 103

Pali Canon, 50
Paraplex, 20
Paul, St., 25
Pentateuch, 46, 47, 48
Persephone, 26, 27, 83, 105, 106, 118, 131, 133, 140
Pindar, 103, 105, 108
Pistis Sophia, 20, 70, 71
Plato, 35, 59, 103, 108, 112n, 117, 124, 145, 147
Pleroma, 54, 55, 127
Pliny, 112
Plotinus, 145
Polydeuces, 105
Porphyry, 117, 119
Proclus, 103, 111, 112n, 119, 123
Prometheus, 28
Psellus, 123
Psyche, 122n, 131
Pythagoras, 145

Qabalah, 14, 17, 21, 27, 28, 29, 44, 54, 59, 62, 63, 64, 69, 82, 83, 84, 92, 116, 127–134
Qesheth, 139, 141
Qlippoth, 138, 141

Ra, 67, 85, 86, 88, 89, 91, 92, 93, 94, 95, 96, 97, 101, 102, 103, 114, 131
Rebirth, 27, 29, 83, 97, 99, 102, 103, 115, 134, 137, 142, 145
Regardie, I., 63, 65, 66, 68n, 78
Resurrection, 43, 84, 97, 115, 135, 137, 140, 142
Rexroth, K., 29
Ritual, 17, 26, 63, 68, 69, 72, 122, 136, 137, 142
Rohde, E., 106, 107
Rosenkreutz, Christian, 142
Rosicrucians, 29
Ruach, 64, 140
Russell, G., ('A.E.'), 60, 61, 62

Sabians, 41
Santayana, G., 17
Sargon II, 46
Sartre, J-P., 35–36
Saturn, 130
Scholem, G., 127, 128n, 133
Set, 84–85n, 101, 137
Shamanism, 17, 31, 32, 33, 34, 103, 104, 107, 111, 113, 114, 116, 134

Simonists, 52
Skinner., S., 82n
Solomon, 46, 115
Spare, A. O., 65
Spinoza, 145
Spiro, M., 15, 17, 18
Statius, 103
Stella Matutina, 63
Stevenson, Dr. I., 151
Suidas, 112
Surrealism, 65
Swedenborg, E., 114

Tanguy, Y., 65
Tarot, 27, 133
Tart, C., 111
Theosophy, 29
Theurgy, 66, 84, 111, 117, 118, 120, 121, 122, 125
Thoth, 87, 88, 89, 101, 130, 141
Thothmes, 45
Tiphareth, 27, 29, 34, 67, 73, 74, 76, 77, 129, 130, 132, 133, 134, 137, 141, 142
Torah, 47
Traherne, T., 59, 62
Tree of Life, 28, 29, 33, 34, 63, 77, 83, 116, 127, 129, 130, 137, 138, 140, 142

Tuat, 86, 87, 89, 90, 92, 93, 97, 99, 101, 104, 114, 134, 135, 136
Tylor, E., 16

Underworld, 26, 27, 86, 98, 103, 104, 107, 111, 140
Uranography, 82, 83

Valentinians, 52
Vaughan, The Works of Thomas, 29n
Venus, 89, 131
Virgil, 103, 107, 125

Waite, A. E., 129
Walker, K., 49

Yaqui, 33, 34
Yesod, 27, 65, 75, 76, 130, 132, 137, 140
Yetzirah, 64, 66, 132
Yoga, 50

Zarathustra, 39, 40, 41, 58
Zeus, 26, 105, 119, 125, 131
Zimmer, H., 50
Zohar, 21, 69, 127, 128
Zurvan, 40, 116